MORE
FAST CAKES

MORE
FAST CAKES

by
Mary Berry

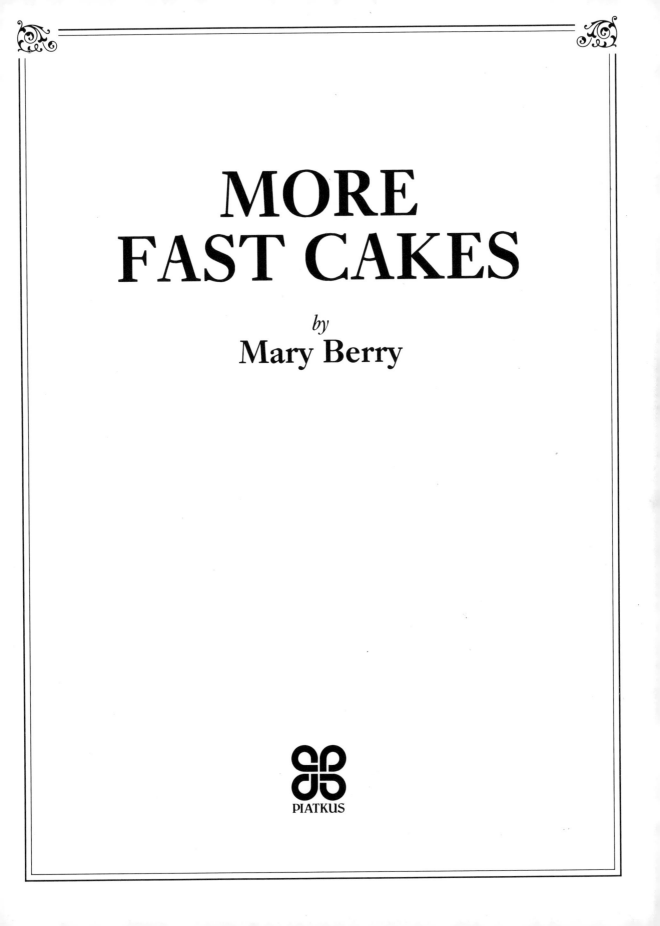

PIATKUS

© 1985 Mary Berry

First published in 1985 by
Judy Piatkus (Publishers) Ltd, London

British Library Cataloguing in Publication Data

Berry, Mary, 1935–
    More fast cakes.
    1. Cake
    I. Title
    641.8'653   TX771

    ISBN 0–86188–362–4

Edited by Susan Fleming
Designed by Susan Ryall
Photography by John Lee

Typeset by Phoenix Photosetting, Chatham
Printed and bound by Mackays of Chatham Ltd

CONTENTS

ILLUSTRATIONS

ACKNOWLEDGEMENTS

A big thank-you to my assistant Debbie Woolhead for her meticulous help with recipe development and testing. It has been a joy to have the cake tin full of such interesting goodies over the past few months.

INTRODUCTION

You might well ask why *more* fast cakes? My previous book on cakes proved exceedingly popular. Only recently in the garden centre, the lady helping me said, 'I must tell you how my family enjoy that fruit cake with the marmalade in it. The children love that Chocolate Juliette too.' She continued with, 'So when's the next cake book coming? And don't forget to put some pictures in it, I like to know exactly what I am aiming at!'

Thus *More Fast Cakes*, and the idea is, again, to give simple, quickly made, delicious cakes, biscuits and breads to please the family. Once more, I have avoided using fancy-shaped tins or long-winded methods. Almost all the recipes are the sort that you weigh the ingredients straight into the mixing bowl and beat until just mixed.

Most of them are easy enough for the children to make, and I always like to encourage them. Both boys and girls enjoy baking, and are so proud when it comes to presenting the results. But I hope you *all* enjoy the book!

BETTER BAKING

The following hints, covering every aspect of baking cakes and biscuits, will be helpful and should ensure successful results every time.

Check your equipment and ingredients
Make sure you have everything you need before you start. The cake tin or tins, all the ingredients needed – and don't improvise with ingredients unless you've tried the recipe at least once before.

In an emergency, make your own cake tin
Sometimes you need a size or shape of cake tin that you haven't got. I sometimes improvise by moulding a double thickness of aluminium foil over the *outside* of the appropriate sized soufflé dish, straight-sided glass bowl or biscuit tin, trim off any surplus from the top, and then carefully stand it on a flat metal baking sheet. Brush the inside of the home-made tin generously with melted lard.

Choosing the recipe to make
Try one that the family are bound to enjoy. If you know it is all going to be eaten

on the day it is made you can choose a fairly economical one that wouldn't keep (such as rock cakes). If you want it to last for some time in the cake tin choose a rich one like Cherry and Walnut Cake. If you know that one of your family or one of your friends loathe coconut, ginger or banana then (obviously!) avoid these flavours.

Check you have time to make the recipe
This should be easy with these recipes as I have put the preparation and baking times. Do remember though that your preparation time could be longer if you have to chop the almonds or defrost some cream from the freezer to fill a sponge.

I have found that you can split the preparation and baking of recipes such as Victoria sponges, fruit cakes, teabreads and shortbread type biscuits, to fit in with your day. Very often I prepare the mixture for Victoria sandwiches and then find that I have an unexpectedly long phone call and there is no time to bake them before, say, fetching the children from school. I simply put the mixture in the tins and then bake them when I get back. They seem to rise just as well. Biscuits and shortbread can indeed improve by being left to chill in the fridge before baking. Recipes that you must prepare and then bake straightaway are whisked sponges, meringues and any recipes with beaten egg whites folded in at the end of the recipe.

Lining the cake tin
You will know whether your own cake tins stick or not, but I prefer to buy loose-bottomed round cake and sandwich tins or to line an ordinary cake tin with greased greaseproof paper. It helps to keep cut-out discs of greaseproof paper cut to the size of your most used sponge sandwich tins together in a bag in a drawer ready to use. It is maddening to have a cake stick to a tin, so I consider it well worth bothering to take care and line them first.

Preparing baking sheets for meringues and sugary items that really stick
Line with silicone non-stick paper (Bakewell). After use brush sugar off the paper and use again and again.

Storing tins and equipment
Anything that would rust is best kept in a dry warm cupboard. Store cake tins one inside the other. Baking sheets and Swiss roll tins are best stored vertically between two divisions as you would store tea trays.

Marking tin sizes and capacities
Scratch the diameter measurements on the bottom of cake tins and the sizes of Swiss roll tins and meat or roasting tins used for tray cakes. It saves measuring every time. I also write the capacities on the base of porcelain and ovenglass

dishes with a freezer or ovenproof marker pen – such a help when it comes to making a flan, and you wonder whether it will take a certain amount of liquid or not.

Choosing, using and storing your cake ingredients

Flour I always use McDougalls flour, and in most cases self-raising. Many of my recipes also use additional baking powder (I use the all-in-one method, which aerates the mixture less than traditional methods). Some recipes also use wholemeal (wholewheat) or granary flour, but these usually replace only half of the white, so that the finished cake is not heavy (the result of using all brown flour). Brown flour is more nutritious than white because it is less refined, and it gives us more fibre which is now recommended for good health. However, it does absorb more water or liquid than white flour, so more liquid is added in these recipes, and extra baking powder is also added to make them rise sufficiently.

I always use Borwicks baking powder as this is what my excellent village shop stocks.

Eggs All of the recipes use size 2 eggs (large 2 oz) which give good results. I always find the best results are from eggs which are left out of the fridge a little while before using them, so that they are at room temperature.

Fats and oils I usually use Blue-Band when soft margarine is required, and Echo block margarine where hard is needed. I use butter where the flavour is important, and the use of margarine would be noticeable. For example in Special Flapjacks or in Burnt Butter Biscuits the buttery flavour is essential, and would be missed if margarine were used instead.

I use sunflower oil in recipes that need oil; as I prefer it to polyunsaturated animal fats.

Sugar In all these recipes I have mostly used unrefined or natural sugars wherever possible. Unrefined demerara sugar is clearly labelled, and the muscovado sugars are both completely natural and have an excellent flavour. If necessary, light and dark soft brown sugars can be substituted for the respective muscovado sugars, but I find there is a noticeable loss of flavour.

It is essential to store all sugars in dry conditions, and icing (powdered) sugar should always be sieved before use. Remember when using golden syrup (light corn syrup) or treacle (molasses), not to be over-generous, as this can upset the balance of ingredients and alter the results of a recipe considerably.

Fruit It is not necessary to wash any dried fruit now, as this is done before packaging and sale to the public. If you can, buy stoned rather than stoneless raisins as they have a much better flavour. However they are often difficult to obtain.

11

Always buy dried apricot pieces to use in a cake, as they will be cheaper than whole dried ones, and it will also save time that is taken up by chopping.

Glacé (candied) cherries usually have a well of syrup in the centre, so it is better to cut them in half or quarters and wash and dry them; this will prevent the fruit sinking in a cake.

Nuts   If a recipe calls for chopped nuts, it is practical to buy broken or pieces of nut rather than whole ones: this not only saves money but time as well.

Store nuts, in separate bags for the different types, in your freezer. In a store cupboard in a warm kitchen, nuts may go off quickly as the fat in them can turn rancid.

Spices   For recipes that use ground spices it is important that they are kept dry. They should be replaced yearly as after this time they tend to lose their flavour and potency to some extent.

Chocolate flavouring   The strongest and most economical way of adding chocolate flavour is to use cocoa powder. In most of the recipes, and for the best results, I sieve the cocoa first, and then mix it until smooth with very hot water.

Mixing with a processor   When using a processor, mix small amounts of mixture at any one time, and take great care not to *over*-mix. When adding dried fruit, it is often best to do this by hand or to just mix for a few seconds as the fruit could easily be chopped up which would spoil the mixture. Processors are marvellous for making pastry, chopping nuts and rubbing in mixtures too.

Baking
Using conventional gas or electric oven   If only one item is being baked at once, bake on the centre shelf. If baking two, either put both on this same shelf, or consult your own manufacturers' cookery book as to shelf positions.

Using fan oven or fan-assisted oven   The baking times and temperatures differ from the conventional ones so do consult the manufacturers' own cookery book and take their advice.

Using a microwave oven   Consult the manufacturers' cookery book for baking methods and times. It is difficult to give advice generally as the electrical output of the different makes and models of microwaves vary. Microwave ovens certainly speed up the baking time but unless the cake is flavoured with chocolate or coffee the appearance is a little pale and disappointing. However, this can be overcome by icing or frosting the cake.

Baking several cakes in one go on different shelves
Even though modern ovens are thermostatically controlled, I find that if several items are baked at once they take longer to cook and in the case of a three-tier wedding cake it can lengthen the time by an hour or so.

To tell when cakes are done

The appearance should be an even colour all over in the case of a plain sponge or fruit cake – pale golden and shrinking away from the sides of the tin. With a large cake test with a warm fine skewer. Gently pierce the centre of the cake through to the bottom of the cake then take it out. If there is a little wet mixture on the skewer, continue cooking for a further 10 minutes or so. Test again and when the skewer comes out clean, then the cake is done. For a sponge press lightly with the finger tip and when it is done it will spring back to its natural shape.

To tell when biscuits and shortbread are done

As a general rule they should be turning a gentle caramel brown colour at the edges. Naturally chocolate-flavoured items will be a darker chocolatey colour at the edges. It is sometimes difficult to tell when a thick shortbread is ready by just looking at the top and it is very important that it is done underneath, so very often I take the tin from the oven and lift a slice carefully out from the centre. The underneath should be very pale golden brown and the middle should look short and cooked, not close and soggy.

Cooling cakes

On taking from the oven, leave in the tin for 10 minutes for a sponge sandwich and 30 minutes for a large cake. Turn out on to a teatowel supported by a plate, then turn the underside on to a cake rack to completely cool. Remove the greaseproof paper, cool completely then store in an airtight tin.

Cooling biscuits

Remove from the oven, leave on the baking tray to firm a little then slip a metal spatula under it and remove to cool on a cake rack. Store in an airtight tin with kitchen paper between the layers.

Freezing

Cakes Freeze as soon as cool. If not iced or frosted wrap carefully in clingfilm then aluminium foil or put in a polythene box. Use within 3 months. If iced or frosted, freeze uncovered until solid then wrap and put in a polythene container and label. Use within 3 months.

Rich fruit cakes can be made several months ahead and kept in the freezer, where I find they mature well. Although traditionally not frozen, with today's warm kitchens I find it a good idea.

Storing ingredients

Store in a dry cupboard in logical sections, keeping the various flours, sugars and fruits together. Leave the flours in the bags they come in, and the sugars as well, unless you wish to decant the ones you use most – ie caster (very fine granulated) sugar. I also keep a separate jar of caster sugar with added vanilla pods so that I always have vanilla sugar on hand for flavouring. If you buy goods in bulk such as 7 lb/3 kg bags of dried fruit or large bags of flaked (slivered) almonds, keep small amounts in the store cupboard and freeze the remainder in polythene bags for up to a couple of years.

Read the recipe

It's very important to do this, even though you may feel you know the method – especially the first time of making. Gather the ingredients together, weighing them carefully, and ticking the items off in pencil if you like. This way you don't forget to add the sugar! Prepare the tin and set the oven then go ahead and make the recipe.

Mixing the recipe

All-in-one method   I have tried to use this whenever possible because it is fast and effective. Take a large roomy bowl, put in all the ingredients and beat until well mixed. Because this method needs less effort and beating than the traditional creaming method in most recipes, a little baking powder is added to compensate for the air not incorporated by the beating. And you should always use soft margarine for this all-in-one method. I find it a marvellously sound way of mixing and I would never go back to the traditional method. If you prefer to use butter instead of soft margarine then you just allow it to become soft and creamy before adding to the all-in-one method.

Mixing with an electric mixer   This saves considerable time. I use both a free-standing and a hand mixer constantly. If you're canny and plan a baking morning, you can start by rubbing in fat to flour for pastry, then make a plain cake then a chocolate cake without washing up the mixer in between!

Biscuits (Cookies)   There is little point in freezing biscuits as most of them keep for a couple of weeks in a tin. However, for longer periods of time, they can be stored in the freezer for up to 3 months. Raw shortbread type of biscuits can be rolled into sausage shapes and frozen. Slices can then be cut from the sausages and when slightly thawed, can be baked freshly as needed.

Coffee

Flavouring   Camp Coffee (liquid coffee extract) gives a good coffee flavour and, being a liquid, it is easy to mix. However, if this is not available, instant coffee mixed with a little hot water and then added gives quite satisfactory results.

ANGLO-AMERICAN EQUIPMENT AND METHOD GLOSSARY

For maximum convenience for American readers, I have added ingredient names and equivalent measures to the actual recipes. The following listings are the most commonly quoted pieces of British equipment and methods, with their American equivalents.

UK	US
baking sheet/tray	cookie sheet
baking tin	baking pan
bun tin	muffin tin
biscuits	cookies
clingfilm	plastic wrap
flan tin	tart pan
frying pan	skillet
greaseproof paper	parchment paper
grill	broiler
grill, to	broil, to
ice, to	glaze, to, or frost, to
icing	frosting
loaf tin	loaf pan
1 lb	small loaf pan
2 lb	large loaf pan
meat tin	roasting pan
palette knife	metal spatula
patty tin	muffin pan
roasting tin	roasting pan
sandwich tin	cake pan
Swiss roll tin	jelly-roll pan
tin	pan

FAMILY CAKES AND TRAYBAKES

Although I put Victoria Sandwich in my previous *Fast Cakes* book, it is a must in every baking book as it is the basic mixture for most cakes. It's so simple and quick to make.

The fastest cakes of all to make are what I call traybakes. They're made in a lined roasting or meat pan or tin, and then iced or frosted in the tin: this means that there's no mopping up of whatever trickles through the rack on to the work surface!

All-in-One Victoria Sandwich

I no longer prepare a Victoria sandwich with all the traditional creaming and folding methods, as this all-in-one method seems to give excellent results every time. *See the photograph facing page 24.*

Making time about 5 minutes
Baking time about 35 minutes

6 oz/175 g (¾ cup) soft margarine
6 oz/175 g (1 cup) caster (very fine granulated) sugar
3 eggs, beaten
6 oz/175 g (1½ cups) self-raising flour
2 level teaspoons baking powder
about 6 tablespoons strawberry or raspberry jam
a little caster (very fine granulated) sugar

Heat the oven to 350°F, 180°C, gas mark 4. Grease and line with greased greaseproof paper two 8-inch/20-cm round sandwich tins.

Measure the margarine, sugar, eggs, flour and baking powder into a large mixing bowl and beat well until thoroughly blended. Divide between the tins, level out evenly and bake in the oven for about 35 minutes until well risen and the top of the sponges spring back when lightly pressed with a finger.

Leave to cool in the tins for a few minutes then turn out, remove the paper and finish cooling on a cake rack.

When completely cold sandwich the cakes together with the jam. Lift on to a serving plate and serve sprinkled with caster sugar.

Variations

Orange and Lemon Sandwich
Add the finely grated rind of 1 orange or 1 lemon to the cake mixture.

Chocolate Sandwich
Blend 2 rounded tablespoons cocoa with 4 tablespoons hot water in the bowl. Cool and then add the remaining ingredients and proceed as above. Fill inside and top with white butter cream – blend 3 oz/75 g (6 tablespoons) soft margarine with 8 oz/225 g (1¼ cups) icing (powdered) sugar, sieved – and decorate with grated chocolate.

Coffee Sandwich
Dissolve 2 heaped teaspoonfuls instant coffee in the beaten eggs before adding to the mixture. Fill centre with coffee butter cream – add 1 tablespoon coffee essence to the white butter cream above – and dredge the top of the sponge with a little sieved icing (powdered) sugar.

Peach Melba Cake

This recipe makes a traditional Victoria sandwich cake that bit more special.

Making time about 15 minutes
Baking time about 25–30 minutes

> *4 oz/100 g (¹/₂ cup) soft margarine*
> *4 oz/100 g (²/₃ cup) caster (very fine granulated) sugar*
> *4 oz/100 g (1 cup) self-raising flour*
> *1 level teaspoon baking powder*
> *2 large eggs, beaten*

Filling and Topping
> *2–3 tablespoons raspberry jam*
> *8-oz/225-g can peach slices, well drained*
> *2 oz/50 g (4 tablespoons) butter, softened*
> *5 oz/150 g (1 cup) icing (powdered) sugar, sieved*

Heat the oven to 350°F, 180°C, gas mark 4. Grease and line with greased greaseproof paper two 7-inch/17.5-cm sandwich tins.

Measure all the ingredients for the cake into a large mixing bowl and beat well until thoroughly blended. Divide the mixture evenly between the two tins and level the tops. Bake in the oven for about 25–30 minutes until beginning to shrink from the sides of the tins and the tops spring back when lightly pressed with a finger. Remove from the oven and turn out on to a cake rack to cool, removing the paper.

When completely cool, spread one of the cakes with jam and arrange the peach slices on top, leaving a few for decoration. Lift the other cake on top and spread with a thin layer of butter icing (frosting) – made by beating together the butter and sugar until smooth. Decorate the cake with the reserved peach slices. Serve in slices.

St Clements Sandwich

If liked, decorate with a little glacé icing (basic glaze), but I think I prefer this sandwich cake served sprinkled with caster sugar.

Making time about 10 minutes
Baking time about 25 minutes

4 oz/100 g (½ cup) soft margarine
4 oz/100 g (⅔ cup) caster (very fine granulated) sugar
finely grated rind of 1 small orange
finely grated rind of 1 lemon
2 eggs, beaten
4 oz/100 g (1 cup) self-raising flour
1 teaspoon baking powder
4 tablespoons lemon curd
a little caster (very fine granulated) sugar to sprinkle on top

Heat the oven to 350°F, 180°C, gas mark 4. Grease and line with greased greaseproof paper two 7-inch/17.5-cm round sandwich tins.

Measure all the ingredients, except the lemon curd, into a bowl and beat well until thoroughly blended. Divide between the prepared tins and level out evenly. Bake in the oven for about 25 minutes until well risen and the top of the sponge springs back when lightly pressed with a finger. Leave to cool in the tin for a few minutes, then turn out, remove the paper and finish cooling on a cake rack.

When cold, sandwich the two cakes together with the lemon curd, lift on to a serving plate, and sprinkle with a little caster sugar just before serving.

Fast, Easy Genoese Sponge

This is a tricky sponge to make in the traditional way: the added melted butter so often makes the mixture separate. But this recipe (dating back to my college days) always works: the page in my book is tatty and torn as I use it again and again whenever I need an extra special sponge cake that keeps well. It makes a glorious dessert cake which should be served chilled.

Making time for the sponge about 15 minutes
   with filling or topping about a further 10 minutes
Baking time 50 minutes

   5 eggs
   5 oz/150 g (³⁄4 cup) caster (very fine granulated) sugar
   4 oz/100 g (1 cup) self-raising flour
   4 tablespoons sunflower oil

Heat the oven to 325°F, 160°C, gas mark 3. Grease and line with greased greaseproof paper two 8-inch/20-cm sandwich tins.

Break the eggs into a large mixing bowl, add the sugar, and whisk with an electric or rotary hand whisk until the mixture is thick and the whisk leaves a trail when it is lifted out. (If using a hand whisk the whisking is speeded up if the sugar is warmed first.) Sift a little of the flour gently on the surface of the egg mixture, fold it in gently with a metal tablespoon then continue in this way until all the flour is included. Lastly fold in the oil. Gently turn into the prepared tins. Bake in the oven for about 50 minutes until the mixture is well risen and shrinking away from the sides of the tins. Cool slightly, ease the edge of the sponges with a metal spatula, and turn out on to a cake rack to cool.

 Fill with whipped cream and hulled strawberries and raspberries, or a filling of choice. Chill.

Chocolate and Date Cake

This is a rich dark chocolate cake, which is best eaten on the day it is made. The dates are delicious chopped into the topping.

Making time about 30 minutes
Baking time about 35 minutes

2 rounded tablespoons cocoa, sieved
3 tablespoons boiling water
6 oz/175 g (³/4 cup) soft margarine
6 oz/175 g (1 cup) caster (very fine granulated) sugar
2 eggs, beaten
8 oz/225 g (2 cups) self-raising flour
1 level teaspoon baking powder
4 fl oz/120 ml (¹/2 cup) milk

Filling and Topping
1 level tablespoon cocoa, sieved
1 tablespoon boiling water
¹/2 oz/15 g (1 tablespoon) butter, softened
6 oz/175 g (1 cup) icing (powdered) sugar, sieved
2 oz/50 g (¹/2 cup) dates, very finely chopped
a few drops water

Heat the oven to 350°F, 180°C, gas mark 4. Grease and line with greased greaseproof paper two 8-inch/20-cm round sandwich tins.

Mix the cocoa and water to a thick paste in a large mixing bowl then add the remaining ingredients for the cake and beat well for about 2 minutes until thoroughly blended. Divide the mixture between the prepared tins and level the tops. Bake in the oven for about 35 minutes until well risen and shrinking away from the sides of the tins. Allow to cool for about 5 minutes in the tins, then turn out, remove the paper and finish cooling on a cake rack.

For the filling and topping, mix the cocoa and water to a paste in a mixing bowl then add remaining ingredients and beat well until thoroughly mixed, adding sufficient water to give a spreading consistency. Sandwich the cakes together with half this mixture and use the remainder to spread on top. Mark decoratively with a fork.

Chocolate Button Cake

A fabulous chocolate cake which is quick to make. Store it in the refrigerator.

Making time about 25 minutes
Baking time about 40 minutes

  2 tablespoons cocoa powder
  2 tablespoons hot water
  6 oz/175 g (³/4 cup) soft margarine
  6 oz/175 g (1 cup) caster (very fine granulated) sugar
  3 eggs
  6 oz/175 g (1¹/2 cups) self-raising flour
  1 teaspoon baking powder
  a few drops peppermint essence

Filling and Decoration
  ¹/2 pint/300 ml (1¹/4 cups) whipping (heavy) cream, whipped
  a small packet chocolate buttons (drops)

Heat the oven to 325°F, 160°C, gas mark 3. Grease and line with greased greaseproof paper two 8-inch/20-cm round sandwich tins.

Measure the cocoa and water into the bottom of a large mixing bowl and mix to a smooth paste. Add the remaining ingredients and beat well until thoroughly blended. Divide the mixture between the tins and level out evenly. Bake in the oven for about 40 minutes until well risen and springs back when lightly pressed with a finger.

Leave to cool in the tins for about 5 minutes then turn out, remove paper and finish cooling on a cake rack.

Sandwich the cakes together with half the whipped cream and spread the remaining cream evenly on top. Decorate with chocolate buttons. Serve in slices.

Right: All-in-One Victoria Sandwich with Chocolate and Coffee variations (pages 18–19).

Devil's Food Cake

This is my version of the traditional American recipe, the yoghurt giving a lovely texture.

Making time about 20 minutes
Baking time about 25–30 minutes

    8 oz/225 g (1¹⁄₃ cups) caster (very fine granulated) sugar
    2 oz/50 g (²⁄₃ cup) cocoa, sieved
    5-oz/142-g (²⁄₃ cup) carton natural yoghurt
    4 oz/100 g (¹⁄₂ cup) soft margarine
    4 large eggs, beaten
    8 oz/225 g (2 cups) self-raising flour
    2 level teaspoons baking powder

Filling and Topping
    3 oz/75 g (6 tablespoons) soft margarine
    6 oz/175 g (1 cup) icing (powdered) sugar, sieved
    3 oz/75 g plain (semi-sweet) chocolate, melted
    apricot jam

Heat the oven to 375°F, 190°C, gas mark 5. Grease and line with greased greaseproof paper two 8-inch/20-cm sandwich tins.

Measure all the ingredients for the cake into a large mixing bowl and beat well until thoroughly blended. Divide between the prepared tins and bake in the oven for about 25–30 minutes until well risen: the cakes should be shrinking away from the sides of the tins and the tops should spring back when lightly pressed.

Remove from the oven, leave to cool in the tins for a few minutes then turn out, remove paper and finish cooling on a cake rack.

For the icing, cream the margarine and sugar together until light then stir in the melted chocolate. Sandwich the sponges together with a layer of apricot jam and half the icing. Spread the remaining icing on top, level out evenly and decorate by drawing squiggly lines in the icing with a fork.

Left: Chocolate Cake Batch Bake (page 26).

Chocolate Cake Batch Bake

There are occasions when perhaps you want to make half a dozen cakes for the freezer, charity sale or coffee morning. We made these in round foil containers – 8-inch/20-cm ones with lids – and iced them in the containers. If you like, sandwich a couple together with whipped cream. *See photograph facing page 25.*

Making time 45 minutes
Baking time about 50 minutes

1¼ lb/600 g (5 cups) plain (all-purpose) flour
6 tablespoons cocoa
3 level teaspoons bicarbonate of soda (baking soda)
3 level teaspoons baking powder
15 oz/425 g (2¼ cups) caster (very fine granulated) sugar
6 level tablespoons golden syrup (light corn syrup)
6 eggs, beaten
¾ pint/450 ml (2 cups) sunflower oil
¾ pint/450 ml (2 cups) milk

Topping
6 oz/175 g (¾ cup) butter
4 oz/100g (1⅓ cups) cocoa, sieved
about 6 tablespoons milk
1 lb 2 oz/500 g (3 cups) icing (powdered) sugar, sieved

Heat the oven to 325°F, 160°C, gas mark 3. Lightly grease six 8-inch/20-cm deep round foil freezer containers.

Measure all the ingredients for the cake into a bowl and beat well for about 3 minutes until thoroughly blended. Divide the mixture between the prepared containers and bake in the oven for about 50 minutes or until the cakes spring back when lightly pressed with a finger. If your oven does not have a very big capacity then bake the cakes in two batches. Allow to cool in the containers.

For the topping, melt the butter in a pan, stir in cocoa and cook for a minute. Remove from the heat and stir in the milk and icing sugar. Beat well until smooth, allow to stand until just beginning to set then divide between the cakes and spread on top. Leave to set.

Makes 6 large cakes

Austrian Currant and Cinnamon Cake

A spicy cake, with the honey flavour really coming through. It's not rich, so should be eaten within a few days.

Making time 8 minutes
Baking time 1½ hours

4 oz/100 g (½ cup) soft margarine
2 oz/50 g (⅓ cup) caster (very fine granulated) sugar
2 level tablespoons thick honey
8 oz/225 g (2 cups) self-raising flour
1 level teaspoon baking powder
4 oz/100 g (¾ cup) currants
1 level teaspoon ground cinnamon
¼ pint/150 ml (⅔ cup) milk

Heat the oven to 325°F, 160°C, gas mark 3. Grease and line a 7-inch/17.5-cm deep round cake tin with greased greaseproof paper.

Measure all the ingredients into a mixing bowl and beat well for about 2 minutes until thoroughly blended. Turn into the prepared tin and bake in the oven for about 1½ hours. Test with a warm fine skewer: if the skewer comes out clean, then the cake is done.

Leave to cool in the tin for about 20 minutes, then turn out, remove the paper, and finish cooling on a cake rack.

Farmers Fruitcake

An excellent fruitcake, the semolina giving it a more crunchy texture.

Making time about 10 minutes
Baking time about 1¼ hours

4 oz/100 g (½ cup) soft margarine
4 oz/100 g (1 cup) dark muscovado (brown) sugar
2 eggs, beaten
2 oz/50 g (½ cup) self-raising flour
4 oz/100 g (1 cup) semolina
1 level teaspoon baking powder
6 oz/175 g (¾ cup) mixed dried fruit
2 oz/50 g (½ cup) walnuts, chopped
2 tablespoons milk

Heat the oven to 350°F, 180°C, gas mark 4. Grease and line with greased greaseproof paper a 6-inch/15-cm deep round cake tin.

Measure all the ingredients into a bowl and beat well for about 2 minutes until thoroughly blended. Turn into the prepared tin, level the top and bake in the oven for about 1¼ hours until well risen. Test with a warm fine skewer: if the skewer comes out clean, then the cake is done.

Allow to cool for about 5 minutes in the tin, then turn out and remove paper and finish cooling on a cake rack.

Frugal Cake

A basic and easy family fruitcake which can be made with any dried fruit you have in the cupboard. It's best eaten on the day it is made.

Making time about 10 minutes
Baking time about 1 hour

8 oz/225 g (2 cups) self-raising flour
4 oz/100 g (½ cup) soft margarine
4 oz/100 g (1 cup) light muscovado (brown) sugar
8 oz/225 g (1 cup) mixed dried fruit
2 eggs, beaten
3 tablespoons milk

Topping
1 tablespoon demerara (brown) sugar

Heat the oven to 350°F, 180°C, gas mark 4. Grease and line with greased greaseproof paper a 7-inch/17.5-cm deep round cake tin.

Measure all the ingredients for the cake into a large mixing bowl and beat well until thoroughly blended. Turn into the prepared tin, level the top and sprinkle with demerara sugar. Bake in the oven for about 1 hour. Test with a warm skewer, and if it comes out clean, then the cake is done.

Leave to cool in the tin for about 30 minutes, then turn out, remove the paper, and finish cooling on a cake rack.

Somerset Fruitcake

A spicy fruitcake that will keep well in an airtight tin.

Making time about 10 minutes
Baking time about 1 hour

> *grated rind and juice of 1 orange*
> *sweet cider*
> *4 oz/100 g (1/2 cup) soft margarine*
> *6 oz/175 g (1 1/2 cups) light muscovado (brown) sugar*
> *2 eggs, beaten*
> *8 oz/225 g (2 cups) self-raising flour*
> *1 level teaspoon baking powder*
> *1/2 teaspoon mixed spice (cinnamon, cloves, nutmeg etc)*
> *1/2 teaspoon ground nutmeg*
> *8 oz/225 g (1 2/3 cups) currants*

Heat the oven to 350°F, 180°C, gas mark 4. Grease and line with greased greaseproof paper a 7-inch/17.5-cm deep round cake tin.

Pour the orange juice and rind into a measuring jug and make up to 1/4 pint/150 ml (2/3 cup) with cider. Measure all the remaining ingredients into a large mixing bowl, add the cider and orange juice and beat well until thoroughly mixed. Turn into the prepared tin, level the top and bake in the oven for about 1 hour. Test with a warm fine skewer: if the skewer comes out clean, then the cake is cooked.

Leave to cool in the tin for about 10 minutes then turn out, remove the paper and finish cooling on a cake rack. Serve in slices.

Cherry Cake

Wash the cherries to remove the syrup and then dry thoroughly before adding to the cake mixture.

Making time about 10 minutes
Baking time about 1 hour

8 oz/225 g (1 cup) glacé (candied) cherries, quartered
6 oz/175 g (1½ cups) self-raising flour
1 teaspoon baking powder
6 oz/175 g (¾ cup) soft margarine
6 oz/175 g (1 cup) caster (very fine granulated) sugar
finely grated rind of 1 lemon
3 eggs, beaten
2 oz/50 g (½ cup) semolina
about 3 tablespoons milk

Heat the oven to 350°F, 180°C, gas mark 4. Grease and line with greased greaseproof paper an 8-inch/20-cm deep round cake tin.

Measure all the ingredients into a large mixing bowl and beat well until thoroughly blended. Turn into the prepared tin and level out evenly. Bake in the oven for about 1 hour until well risen and the cake is beginning to shrink away from the sides of the tin.

Leave to cool in the tin for about 10 minutes then turn out and finish cooling on a cake rack.

Cherry and Walnut Cake

To prevent cherries from sinking to the bottom of a cake, rinse the syrup off the halved cherries with cold water then drain well and dry before adding to the cake.

Making time about 10 minutes
Baking time about 1¼ hours

6 oz/175 g (¾ cup) soft margarine
2 oz/50 g (⅓ cup) caster (very fine granulated) sugar
4 oz/100 g (1 cup) light muscovado (brown) sugar
3 eggs, beaten
8 oz/225 g (2 cups) self-raising flour
1 level teaspoon baking powder
4 oz/100 g (½ cup) glacé (candied) cherries, halved
2 oz/50 g (½ cup) walnuts, chopped
grated rind of 1 orange
2 tablespoons milk

Heat the oven to 350°F, 180°C, gas mark 4. Grease and line with greased greaseproof paper a 7-inch/17.5-cm deep round cake tin.

Measure all the ingredients into a large mixing bowl and beat well for about 2 minutes until thoroughly blended. Turn into the prepared tin, level the top and bake in the oven for about 1¼ hours until well risen. Test with a warm fine skewer: if the skewer comes out clean then the cake is done.

Allow to cool in the tin for about 5 minutes then turn out, remove paper, and finish cooling on a cake rack.

Old English Seed Cake

Seed cakes were always popular in the past; this one is a more updated version.

Making time about 10 minutes
Baking time about 1 hour 10 minutes

> *6 oz/175 g (³/₄ cup) soft margarine*
> *4 oz/100 g (²/₃ cup) caster (very fine granulated) sugar*
> *2 eggs, beaten*
> *8 oz/225 g (2 cups) self-raising flour*
> *1 level teaspoon baking powder*
> *1 rounded tablespoon caraway seeds*
> *grated rind of 1 lemon*
> *4 tablespoons milk*

Heat the oven to 350°F, 180°C, gas mark 4. Grease and line a 7-inch/17.5-cm deep round cake tin with greased greaseproof paper.

Measure all the ingredients into a bowl and beat well for about 2 minutes until thoroughly blended. Turn into the prepared tin, level the top and bake in the oven for about 1 hour 10 minutes until well risen and shrinking from the sides of the tin. Test with a warm fine skewer: if the skewer comes out clean then the cake is done.

Allow to cool in the tin for about 10 minutes then turn out, remove paper, and finish cooling on a cake rack.

Whisky Cake

A light cake, which is very moist and not too richly fruited.

Making time 15 minutes
Baking time about 1¼ hours

6 oz/175 g (¾ cup) soft margarine
6 oz/175 g (1 cup) caster (very fine granulated) sugar
6 oz/175 g (1½ cups) self-raising flour
1 level teaspoon baking powder
3 eggs, beaten
6 oz/175 g (1¼ cups) sultanas (golden raisins)
grated rind of 1 lemon
3 tablespoons less expensive whisky

Heat the oven to 350°F, 180°C, gas mark 4. Grease and line with greased greaseproof paper an 8-inch/20-cm deep round cake tin.

Measure all the ingredients, except the whisky, into a large mixing bowl and beat well until thoroughly blended. Turn into the prepared tin, level the top and bake in the oven for about 1¼ hours. Test with a warm fine skewer: if the skewer comes out clean then the cake is done.

Leave to cool in the tin for about 10 minutes, then turn out, remove the paper, turn upside down, sprinkle with whisky, then finish cooling the right way up on a cake rack.

Cider Cake

Best eaten on the day it is prepared or, if there is some left over, heat it through in a warm oven and serve as a pudding with whipped cream.

Making time about 10 minutes
Baking time about 40 minutes

8 oz/225 g (2 cups) self-raising flour
1 level teaspoon baking powder
3 oz/75 g (6 tablespoons) soft margarine
3 oz/75 g (½ cup) caster (very fine granulated) sugar
grated rind of 1 orange
1 egg, beaten
¼ pint/150 ml (⅔ cup) sweet cider

Topping
1 oz/25 g (¼ cup) self-raising flour
2 oz/50 g (⅓ cup) demerara (brown) sugar
1 oz/25 g (2 tablespoons) butter, melted

Heat the oven to 375°F, 190°C, gas mark 5. Grease and line with greased greaseproof paper an 8-inch/20-cm deep round cake tin.

Measure all the cake ingredients into a bowl and beat well until thoroughly blended. Turn into the prepared tin, level the top and prepare the topping.

Mix the flour and sugar in a bowl, add the melted butter and mix thoroughly then sprinkle on top of the cake. Bake in the oven for about 40 minutes until well risen and golden brown. Test with a warm fine skewer: if the skewer comes out clean then the cake is done.

Leave to cool in the tin for about 10 minutes, then turn out, remove the paper and finish cooling on a cake rack. Serve in slices.

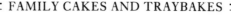

Plain Lemon Cake

A simple cut-and-come-again cake that keeps for a week.

Making time about 10 minutes
Baking time about 1 hour

4 oz/100 g (¹/₂ cup) soft margarine
4 oz/100 g (²/₃ cup) demerara (brown) sugar
5 oz/150 g (1¹/₄ cups) self-raising flour
grated rind and juice of 1 lemon
1 tablespoon golden syrup (light corn syrup)
2 eggs, beaten

Topping
a little demerara (brown) sugar

Heat the oven to 350°F, 180°C, gas mark 4. Grease and line a 7-inch/17.5-cm deep round cake tin with greased greaseproof paper.

Measure all the ingredients into a large mixing bowl and beat well until thoroughly blended. Turn into the prepared tin, level the top and bake in oven for about 1 hour until golden brown. Test with a warm fine skewer: if the skewer comes out clean, then the cake is done.

Sprinkle with a little demerara sugar then leave to cool in the tin for about 10 minutes. Turn out, peel off paper, and finish cooling on a cake rack.

Moist Orange Cake

If you don't happen to have a spare orange in your fruit bowl then use a lemon instead.

Making time about 20 minutes
Baking time about 1 hour

4 oz/100 g (1 cup) self-raising flour
2 oz/50 g (½ cup) wholemeal (wholewheat) flour
4 oz/100 g (1 cup) light muscovado (brown) sugar
2 level teaspoons baking powder
grated rind of 1 small, thin-skinned orange
2 eggs, beaten
4 oz/100 g (½ cup) soft margarine
4 tablespoons milk

Topping
6 oz/175 g (1½ cups) icing (powdered) sugar, sieved
juice of ½ orange

Heat the oven to 350°F, 180°C, gas mark 4. Grease and line with greased greaseproof paper a deep 7-inch/17.5-cm round cake tin.

Measure all the ingredients for the cake into a large mixing bowl and beat well until thoroughly blended. Turn into the prepared tin, level the top and bake in the oven for about 1 hour until well risen and golden brown. Remove from the oven and leave to cool for about 15 minutes then turn out of the tin, remove the paper and finish cooling on a cake rack.

For the topping, sieve the icing sugar into a bowl and add sufficient of the orange juice to give a smooth glacé icing (basic glaze). Spread evenly over the top of the cake, allow to set, then serve cake in slices.

Coffee and Ginger Traybake

Lovely and moist, this cake keeps well in an airtight tin.

Making time about 15 minutes
Baking time about 1¼ hours

3 good teaspoons ground ginger
4 oz/100 g (1 cup) wholemeal (wholewheat) flour
4 oz/100 g (1 cup) self-raising flour
1 level teaspoon baking powder
4 oz/100 g (½ cup) hard margarine
3 tablespoons black treacle (molasses)
4 tablespoons golden syrup (light corn syrup)
2 oz/50 g (½ cup) light muscovado (brown) sugar
¼ pint/150 ml (⅔ cup) milk
2 eggs, beaten

Icing (Basic Glaze)
8 oz/225 g (1⅔ cups) icing (powdered) sugar, sieved
2 teaspoons coffee essence
about 1½ tablespoons water

Heat the oven to 325°F, 160°C, gas mark 3. Grease and line a 6½ × 8½-inch/16 × 21-cm roasting tin with greased greaseproof paper.

Measure the ginger, flours and baking powder into a bowl. Put the margarine, black treacle, golden syrup and sugar in a pan and heat gently until the margarine has melted. Add the melted mixture to the flour with the milk and eggs and beat well until thoroughly blended. Pour into the prepared tin and bake in the oven for about 1¼ hours until well risen and the top springs back when lightly pressed with a finger. Leave to cool in the tin for a few moments then turn out, remove paper and finish cooling on a cake rack.

For the icing, measure the icing sugar into a bowl, add the coffee essence and sufficient water to give a smooth icing. Spread evenly over the top of the cake and leave to set. Cut into 18 squares to serve.

Makes 18 squares

Chocolate Tray Bake

Ice the cake whilst it is still in the tin. This saves a lot of cleaning up of your work surface if some of the icing runs off then sets. *See the photograph facing page 48.*

Making time about 15 minutes
Baking time about 40 minutes

3 level tablespoons cocoa powder
3 tablespoons hot water
6 oz/175 g (³/4 cup) soft margarine
8 oz/225 g (2 cups) self-raising flour
2 level teaspoons baking powder
6 oz/175 g (1 cup) caster (very fine granulated) sugar
3 eggs, beaten
3 tablespoons milk

Icing (Frosting)
3 oz/75 g (6 tablespoons) hard margarine
2 oz/50 g (²/3 cup) cocoa powder, sieved
8 oz/225 g (1²/3 cups) icing (powdered) sugar, sieved
2 tablespoons water

Heat the oven to 350°F, 180°C, gas mark 4. Grease and line with greased greaseproof paper a 9 × 12-inch/22.5 × 30-cm roasting tin.

Measure the cocoa and water into the bottom of a large mixing bowl, and mix well until smooth. Add the remaining ingredients for the cake and beat well until thoroughly blended. Turn into the prepared tin, level out evenly and bake in the oven for about 40 minutes until well risen and the top of the cake springs back when lightly pressed with a finger. Remove from the oven and leave to cool in the tin.

For the icing, melt the margarine in a pan then add the cocoa and cook for a minute. Remove from the heat, stir in the icing sugar and water, and beat well until smooth. Leave to cool until a spreading consistency then spread evenly over the top of the cake. When the icing has set, divide the cake into about 20 pieces and carefully lift out of the tin.

Makes about 20 pieces

American Chocolate Oat Slice

This slice is still quite soft when it comes out of the oven so leave to become quite cold before lifting the fingers out of the tin.

Making time about 15 minutes
Baking time about 30 minutes

4 oz/100 g (¹/₂ cup) butter, softened
6 oz/175 g (1¹/₂ cups) light muscovado brown sugar
1 egg, beaten
5 oz/150 g (1¹/₄ cups) self-raising flour
1 level teaspoon baking powder
5 oz/150 g (2 cups) porridge (rolled) oats

Filling
6 oz/175 g plain (semi-sweet) chocolate
6.91-oz/196-g can condensed milk
¹/₂ oz/15 g (1 tablespoon) butter
2 oz/50 g (¹/₂ cup) chopped walnuts

Heat the oven to 350°F, 180°C, gas mark 4. Lightly butter a 7 × 11-inch/17.5 × 27.5-cm deep Swiss roll tin.

Measure the butter and sugar into a large mixing bowl and cream together until light. Gradually beat in the egg, then work in the flour, baking powder and oats. Leave on one side whilst making the filling.

For the filling, measure the chocolate, contents of the can of condensed milk, butter and the chopped walnuts into a bowl and heat gently over a pan of simmering water until the chocolate and butter have melted. Remove from the heat and beat well until thoroughly blended.

Press half the oat mixture evenly into the bottom of the prepared tin, then top with the chocolate mixture followed by the remaining oat mixture. Use a fork to spread this top layer out evenly. Don't worry if some of the chocolate mixture seeps through the top layer as this gives a lovely marbled effect when baked.

Bake in the oven for about 30 minutes until pale golden brown. Remove from the oven and leave to cool in the tin then cut into 20 fingers.

Makes 20 fingers

Fresh Date Slices

Either serve these cold in fingers with icing or frosting, or serve warm, *without* icing, as a pudding with cream.

Making time about 15 minutes
Baking time about 30 minutes

3 oz/75 g (³/4 cup) self-raising flour
2 oz/50 g (¹/2 cup) wholemeal (wholewheat) flour
1 level teaspoon baking powder
5 oz/150 g (1¹/4 cups) light muscovado (brown) sugar
6 oz/175 g fresh dates, stoned, skinned and chopped
4 oz/100 g (¹/2 cup) butter, melted
1 egg, beaten
a few drops vanilla essence (extract)

Icing (Basic Glaze)
1 level tablespoon cocoa powder, sieved
water to mix
4 oz/100 g (³/4 cup) icing (powdered) sugar, sieved

Heat the oven to 350°F, 180°C, gas mark 4. Grease a 7 × 11-inch/ 17.5 × 27.5-cm Swiss roll tin.

Measure all the ingredients for the date slices into a large mixing bowl and beat well until thoroughly blended. Turn into the tin, level out evenly and bake in the oven for about 30 minutes. Leave to cool in the tin.

For the icing, measure the cocoa and 1 tablespoon *hot* water into a bowl and stir until blended and smooth. Leave to cool then work in the icing sugar, adding a little more cold water if necessary to give a coating consistency. Pour the icing over the cake while it is still warm and then leave to become quite cold before cutting and serving in fingers.

Makes 12 fingers

Crunchy Date Squares

These always disappear quite quickly out of the cake tin. If you find you haven't got 8 oz/225 g dates in your store cupboard then make up the quantity with currants or raisins.

Making time about 15 minutes
Baking time about 30 minutes

6 oz/175 g (1½ cups) self-raising flour
6 oz/175 g (1½ cups) semolina
6 oz/175 g (¾ cup) soft margarine
3 oz/75 g (½ cup) demerara (brown) sugar

Filling
8 oz/225 g (1¼ cups) dates, finely chopped
3 oz/75 g (¾ cup) dark muscovado (brown) sugar
juice of 1 lemon
1 level teaspoon mixed spice (cinnamon, cloves, nutmeg etc.)

Heat the oven to 375°F, 190°C, gas mark 5. Lightly grease a 7.5 × 11-inch/17.5 × 27.5-cm Swiss roll tin.

Measure the flour and semolina into a bowl and rub in the margarine until the mixture resembles fine breadcrumbs. Stir in the sugar. Spread half of this mixture into the bottom of the prepared tin and press down firmly to cover the base of the tin evenly.

For the filling, mix all the ingredients together until thoroughly blended. Spread on top of the mixture in the tin. Spoon remaining crumble mixture on top, level out evenly and press down gently with the back of a spoon. Bake in the oven for about 30 minutes until golden brown. Cut into 18 squares then leave to cool in the tin before lifting out with a metal spatula.

Makes 18 squares

Sultana Slices

These rich fruit slices are delicious cold, or warm with a blob of whipped cream.

Making time about 25 minutes
Baking time 35–40 minutes

4 oz/100 g (1 cup) wholemeal (wholewheat) flour
4 oz/100 g (1 cup) plain (all-purpose) flour
4 oz/100 g (½ cup) margarine
about 4 tablespoons water

Filling
4 oz/100 g (½ cup) margarine
1 level dessertspoon golden syrup (1 level tablespoon light corn syrup)
4 oz/100 g (1 cup) light muscovado (brown) sugar
12 oz/350 g (2½ cups) sultanas (golden raisins)
1 oz/25 g (¼ cup) plain (all-purpose) flour
juice of ½ lemon
milk and caster (very fine granulated) sugar to glaze

Heat the oven to 350°F, 180°C, gas mark 4. Lightly grease a 7-inch/17.5-cm square baking tin.

Measure the flours into a bowl and rub in the margarine until the mixture resembles fine breadcrumbs. Bind together with sufficient water to give a firm dough. Divide the pastry in two. Roll out one half and use to line the base of the tin.

For the filling, heat the margarine and syrup in a pan over a low heat until the margarine has melted. Remove from the heat and stir in the sugar, sultanas, flour and lemon juice until thoroughly mixed. Spoon the mixture into the pastry case and level out evenly. Roll out the remaining piece of pastry large enough to form a lid. Brush the edges with a little water, lift the pastry lid on top of the fruit filling. Seal the edges and trim off any excess pastry. Make a few diagonal slits in the top of the pastry with a sharp knife. Glaze with a little milk, sprinkle with caster sugar and bake in the oven for 35–40 minutes until golden brown. Leave to cool in the tin, then cut into 8 slices to serve.

Makes about 8 slices

Almond and Candied Peel Squares

Not a good keeping cake, this is best eaten on the day it is prepared.

Making time 10 minutes
Baking time about 30 minutes

2 oz/50 g (4 tablespoons) soft margarine
4 oz/100 g (²/₃ cup) caster (very fine granulated) sugar
3 eggs, beaten
4 oz/100 g (1 cup) self-raising flour
4 oz/100 g semolina
1 level teaspoon baking powder
1 level teaspoon almond essence (extract)
2 oz/50 g (¹/₄ cup) candied peel, chopped
2 tablespoons milk

To top
1 oz/25 g (¹/₄ cup) flaked (slivered) almonds

Heat the oven to 350°F, 180°C, gas mark 4. Grease and line a 6½ × 8½-inch/16 × 21-cm small roasting tin with greased greaseproof paper.

Measure all the ingredients into a bowl and beat well until thoroughly blended. Turn on to the prepared tin, level the top, sprinkle with flaked almonds and bake in the oven for about 30 minutes until pale golden brown.

Allow to cool in the tin then turn out, remove paper and divide into 16 squares.

Makes 16 squares

Chocolate Fudge Squares

Everybody seems to adore chocolate. These squares have a thick rich topping of icing and are always a great favourite.

Making time about 20 minutes
Baking time about 40 minutes

3 level tablespoons cocoa
3 tablespoons hot water
6 oz/175 g (³/4 cup) soft margarine
6 oz/175 g (1 cup) caster (very fine granulated) sugar
3 eggs, beaten
6 oz/175 g (1¹/2 cups) self-raising flour
2 level teaspoons baking powder

Topping
3 oz/75 g (6 tablespoons) butter
2 oz/50 g (²/3 cup) cocoa, sieved
4 tablespoons milk
8 oz/225 g (1²/3 cups) icing (powdered) sugar, sieved

Heat the oven to 350°F, 180°C, gas mark 4. Grease and line with greased greaseproof paper a small 11 × 9-inch/27.5 × 22.5-cm roasting tin.

Measure the cocoa into a large mixing bowl and blend with the hot water. Add the remaining cake ingredients and beat well until thoroughly blended. Turn into the prepared tin, level the top and bake in the oven for about 40 minutes until the sides of the cake are beginning to shrink from the sides of the tin, and the top of the cake springs back when lightly pressed with a finger. Turn out, remove paper and leave to cool on a cake rack.

For the topping, melt the butter in a small pan, add the cocoa and cook for a minute. Remove from the heat and stir in the milk and icing sugar. Beat well until smooth then leave, stirring occasionally, until of a spreading consistency. Spread thickly and evenly over the top of the cake. Leave to set and cut into squares to serve.

Makes about 20 squares

Sticky Ginger Buns

These ginger buns – the stem ginger and golden syrup giving them a lovely flavour – are best eaten on the day they are made.

Making time about 20 minutes
Baking time about 15–20 minutes

>*6 oz/175 g (1½ cups) self-raising flour*
>*3 oz/75 g (6 tablespoons) soft margarine*
>*3 oz/75 g (½ cup) caster (very fine granulated) sugar*
>*2 level tablespoons golden syrup (light corn syrup)*
>*1 level teaspoon baking powder*
>*1 level teaspoon ground ginger*
>*1 oz/25 g (2 tablespoons) stem (preserved) ginger, drained and chopped*
>*1 large egg, beaten*
>*2 tablespoons milk*

Icing (Basic Glaze)
>*4 oz/100 g (¾ cup) icing (powdered) sugar, sieved*
>*about 1 tablespoon syrup from the jar of stem (preserved) ginger*

Heat the oven to 375°F, 190°C, gas mark 5. Arrange 24 paper cases in patty tins.

Measure all the bun mixture ingredients into a large mixing bowl and beat well until thoroughly blended. Spoon a good teaspoonful of the mixture into each of the paper cases and bake in the oven for about 15–20 minutes until golden brown. Remove from the oven and leave to cool on a cake rack.

For the icing, measure the icing sugar into a bowl and work in sufficient syrup to give a smooth glacé icing. Spread a little on top of each bun and allow to set.

Makes 24 buns

Peppermint Cream Cakes

Don't be over-generous with the peppermint essence – 3 drops are just enough to give the icing a delicate peppermint flavour.

Making time about 20 minutes
Baking time about 10 minutes

> *1 tablespoon cocoa powder*
> *1 tablespoon hot water*
> *4 oz/100 g (½ cup) soft margarine*
> *4 oz/100 g (⅔ cup) caster (very fine granulated) sugar*
> *3 oz/75 g (¾ cup) self-raising flour*
> *1 teaspoon baking powder*
> *2 eggs, beaten*

Icing (Basic Glaze)
> *8 oz/225 g (1⅔ cups) icing (powdered) sugar, sieved*
> *about 2 tablespoons cold water*
> *2–3 drops peppermint essence (extract)*
> *2–3 drops green food colouring*

Decoration
> *chocolate peppermints*

Heat the oven to 400°F, 200°C, gas mark 6. Arrange 18 paper cases in patty tins.

Measure the cocoa and hot water into a large mixing bowl and blend together until smooth. Add the remaining ingredients for the cakes and beat well until thoroughly blended. Spoon a good teaspoonful of the mixture into each of the paper cases. Bake in the oven for about 10 minutes until well risen and the tops of the sponges spring back when lightly pressed with a finger. Remove paper cases from patty tins, and leave to cool on a cake rack.

For the icing, measure the icing sugar into a bowl and add sufficient water to give a smooth coating consistency. Stir in the peppermint essence and food colouring and mix well. Spread a little of the icing on top of each cake and decorate with either a whole or half a chocolate peppermint.

Makes 18 small cakes

Coburg Cakes

These are pretty little cakes which are served with the almond side facing upwards.

Making time about 10 minutes
Baking time about 20 minutes

> 3 oz/75 g (6 tablespoons) soft margarine
> 1 level tablespoon golden syrup (light corn syrup)
> 2 eggs, beaten
> 2 oz/50 g (1/3 cup) caster (very fine granulated) sugar
> 5 oz/150 g (1 1/4 cups) self-raising flour
> 1 teaspoon ground ginger
> 1 level teaspoon baking powder
> about 1 oz/25 g (1/4 cup) flaked (slivered) almonds

Heat the oven to 350°F, 180°C, gas mark 4. Lightly grease two patty tins.

Measure the margarine, syrup, eggs, sugar, flour, ginger and baking powder into a bowl and beat well until thoroughly blended. Put a few flakes of almond into the bottom of each patty tin. Spoon a good teaspoonful of the mixture on top and bake in the oven for about 20 minutes or until the cakes are well risen and the mixture has shrunk away from the sides of the tin a little.

Allow to cool in the tins for a few moments then carefully lift out with a metal spatula and finish cooling on a cake rack.

Makes 24 small cakes

Right: Chocolate Tray Bake (page 39).

Old-Fashioned Rock Cakes

These cakes take no time at all to prepare, and are wonderful to serve if you have unexpected guests. They are best eaten when freshly made.

Making time about 10 minutes
Baking time about 15 minutes

> *8 oz/225 g (2 cups) self-raising flour*
> *1 good teaspoon baking powder*
> *1/2 level teaspoon ground mixed spice (cinnamon, cloves, nutmeg, etc.)*
> *4 oz/100 g (1/2 cup) soft margarine*
> *2 oz/50 g (1/3 cup) demerara (brown) sugar*
> *4 oz/100 g (1/2 cup) mixed dried fruit*
> *1 egg, beaten*
> *about 1 tablespoon milk*
> *a little extra demerara (brown) sugar, to top*

Heat the oven to 400°F, 200°C, gas mark 6. Lightly grease two large baking sheets.

Measure the flour, baking powder and mixed spice into a bowl and rub in the margarine until the mixture resembles fine breadcrumbs. Add the sugar and fruit then mix to a stiff dough with the egg and milk, adding a little extra milk if the dough is too dry.

Spoon the mixture in rough mounds on the baking sheets using two teaspoons, sprinkle with a little demerara sugar and bake in the oven for about 15 minutes until just beginning to turn golden brown. Carefully lift off the baking sheet with a metal spatula and leave to cool on a cake rack.

Makes 12 rock cakes

Left: Fresh Cream Sponge Cake (page 62) and Honey and Almond Swiss Roll (page 65).

SPECIAL OCCASION CAKES

Most people seem to enjoy a rich fruitcake for a celebration cake, and the one with many size variations which follows is very moist: the fruit is soaked in orange juice which plumps up the fruit and gives an extra fruity flavour. To go with this cake, I always used to make my own marzipan or almond paste, but I now find that there are many good ones available commercially (I choose a natural pale coloured one). To accompany the fruitcake size 'table', I give some ideas how much almond paste and fondant icing will be needed for varying sizes of cake.

My favourites in this section, apart from the Rich Fruitcake are Coffee Walnut Gâteau, Wimbledon Cake, Fresh Cream Sponge Cake and – for a really special occasion – Celebration Ice-Cream Cake.

Method for Rich Fruitcake

Put the mixed dried fruit and chopped cherries into a large ice-cream container or polythene box, and pour the orange juice over. Cover with a lid and leave for at least 3 days, stirring occasionally.

Measure the margarine and sugar into a large mixing bowl and cream well until light. Lightly beat the eggs and add to the creamed mixture a little at a time until all has been added then work in the chopped walnuts, self-raising flour, wholemeal (wholewheat) flour and the spices until thoroughly blended. Finally, stir in the soaked fruit and mix well until evenly mixed. (With large quantities of mixture it may be easiest to use your hands.)

Heat the oven to 300°F, 150°C, gas mark 2. Grease and line the appropriate sized tin with greased greaseproof paper. Spoon the mixture into the prepared tin and level the top. Bake in the oven for the length of time suggested on the chart, reducing the oven temperature as suggested. If making several tiers for a cake, the best results are obtained by baking one layer at a time. To test when the cake is done, pierce through the centre of the cake with a warm fine skewer: if it comes out clean then the cake is done. If not, then return to the oven for about a further 15 minutes until cooked. If during cooking the top of the cake begins to get too brown, cover the top of the cake loosely with a piece of foil.

Remove from the oven and leave to cool completely in the tin then turn out, remove and discard the paper, and decorate as required.

Rich Fruitcake

Round tin	**7 inch/17.5 cm**	**8 inch/20 cm**	**9 inch/22.5 cm**	**10 inch/25 cm**	**11 inch/27.5 cm**	**12 inch/30 cm**	**13 inch/32.5 cm**
Square tin	**6 inch/15 cm**	**7 inch/17.5 cm**	**8 inch/20 cm**	**9 inch/22.5 cm**	**10 inch/25 cm**	**11 inch/27.5 cm**	**12 inch/30 cm**
mixed dried fruit	1 lb/450 g (2½ cups)	2 lb/900 g (5 cups)	3 lb/1.3 kg (7½ cups)	4 lb/1.75 kg (10 cups)	5 lb/2.25 kg (12½ cups)	6 lb/2.75 kg (15 cups)	7 lb/3 kg (17½ cups)
glacé (candied) cherries, chopped	2 oz/50 g (¼ cup)	4 oz/100 g (½ cup)	6 oz/175 g (¾ cup)	8 oz/225 g (1 cup)	10 oz/275 g (1¼ cups)	12 oz/350 g (1½ cups)	14 oz/400 g (1¾ cups)
orange juice	2½ fl oz/ 65 ml (⅓ cup)	¼ pint/ 150 ml (½ cup)	good ¼ pint/ 150 ml (⅔ cup)	½ pint/ 300 ml (1¼ cups)	good ½ pint/ 300 ml (1½ cups)	¾ pint/ 450 ml (1¾ cups)	good ¾ pint/ 450 ml (2 cups)
soft margarine	3 oz/75 g (6 tbsp)	6 oz/175 g (¾ cup)	9 oz/250 g (1 cup 2tbsp)	12 oz/350 g (1½ cups)	15 oz/425 g (1¾ cups 2 tbsp)	1 lb 2 oz/500 g (2¼ cups)	1 lb 5 oz/600 g (2½ cups 2 tbsp)
dark muscovado (brown) sugar	3 oz/75 g (⅓ cup)	6 oz/175 g (⅔ cup)	9 oz/250 g (1 cup)	12 oz/350 g (1⅓ cups)	15 oz/425 g (1⅔ cups)	1 lb 2 oz/500 g (2 cups)	1 lb 5 oz/600 g (2⅓ cups)
eggs	2	3	5	6	7	9	10
chopped walnuts	1 oz/25 g (¼ cup)	2 oz/50 g (½ cup)	3 oz/75 g (¾ cup)	4 oz/100 g (1 cup)	5 oz/150 g (1¼ cups)	6 oz/175 g (1½ cups)	7 oz/200 g (1¾ cups)
self-raising flour	1½ oz/40 g (⅓ cup)	3 oz/75 g (⅔ cup)	4½ oz/120 g (1 cup)	6 oz/175 g (1⅓ cups)	7½ oz/212 g (1⅔ cups)	9 oz/250 g (2 cups)	10½ oz/285 g (2⅓ cups)
wholemeal (wholewheat) flour	1½ oz/40 g (⅓ cup)	3 oz/75 g (⅔ cup)	4½ oz/120 g (1 cup)	6 oz/175 g (1⅓ cups)	7½ oz/212 g (1⅔ cups)	9 oz/250 g (2 cups)	10½ oz/285 g (2⅓ cups)
mixed spice (cinnamon, cloves, nutmeg, etc.)	½ tsp	1 tsp	1½ tsp	2 tsp	2½ tsp	3 tsp	3½ tsp
ground nutmeg	½ tsp	1 tsp	1½ tsp	2 tsp	2½ tsp	3 tsp	3½ tsp
Baking time							
300°F, 150°C, gas mark 2	2 hours	2 hours	2 hours	2 hours	2 hours	2 hours	2 hours
then at 275°F, 140°C, gas mark 1	¾ hour	1¼ hours	1½ hours	1¾ hours	2¼ hours	2¾ hours	3 hours
Total Baking time	**2¾ hours**	**3¼ hours**	**3½ hours**	**3¾ hours**	**4¼ hours**	**4¾ hours**	**5 hours**

Almond Paste

When making and decorating rich fruitcakes I now buy almond paste from good bakers or delicatessens. I find the quality is excellent, it doesn't cost any more to buy it then to make it, and it also saves a great deal of time. Here is a table I work to for finding the quantities required.

7 inch/17.5 cm round or	6 inch/15 cm	square takes	1 lb (450 g)	almond paste		
8 inch/20 cm „	„ 7 inch/17.5 cm	„	„ 1½ lb (675 g)	„	„	
9 inch/22.5 cm „	„ 8 inch/20 cm	„	„ 1¾ lb (775 g)	„	„	
10 inch/25 cm „	„ 9 inch/22.5 cm	„	„ 2 lb (900 g)	„	„	
11 inch/27.5 cm „	„ 10 inch/25 cm	„	„ 2¼ lb (1 kg)	„	„	
12 inch/30 cm „	„ 11 inch/27.5 cm	„	„ 2½ lb (1.1 kg)	„	„	
13 inch/32.5 cm „	„ 12 inch/30 cm	„	„ 3 lb (1.3 kg)	„	„	

To almond paste a cake   Brush cake all over with apricot glaze (sieved warmed apricot jam). Knead until soft and pliable then roll out the almond paste until it is 2 inches/5 cm larger than the cake in diameter plus sides. Lift paste on to a rolling pin and unroll on top of the cake. Smooth over with your hands then trim off at the base of the cake. Smooth over with a professional smoother or your hands to give a smooth even surface. Allow to dry out for a few days before icing (frosting).

All-in-One
Fondant Icing (Frosting)

This is the easiest icing I know for decorating special cakes such as wedding cakes, christening cakes and Christmas cakes. It is just rolled out like pastry and moulded over the cake.

about 1 lb 2 oz/500 g (2²/3 cups) icing (powdered) sugar
1 good tablespoon liquid glucose
1 egg white

Sieve the icing sugar into a large mixing bowl, make a well in the centre and add the liquid glucose and the egg white. Work the ingredients together until they form a soft ball then turn on to a work surface sprinkled with extra sieved icing sugar and knead the mixture for a good 5 minutes until really white and smooth. Keep adding a little more sieved icing sugar if the mixture gets a bit sticky. Any colouring can be kneaded in at this stage. Store in the refrigerator wrapped in clingfilm until required. The icing will keep for about 5 days in the refrigerator.

To cover a cake with all-in-one fondant icing Brush the almond-pasted cake all over with a little sherry. Roll out the icing to 2 inches (5 cm) larger than the cake plus sides on a surface sprinkled with sieved icing sugar. Lift with the help of a rolling pin over the cake and smooth over quickly with the hands so that it moulds around the shape of the cake. Cut the excess away from the base of the cake to neaten the edge. Smooth over the top and sides with a professional smoother or the flat side of a gin bottle (which works just as well)! Leave to dry out for 24 hours before decorating.

Quantities of All-in-One Fondant Icing (Frosting)

7 inch/17.5 cm	round or	6 inch/15 cm	square	needs	¾	× the recipe
8 inch/20 cm	„	„ 7 inch/17.5 cm	„	„	1	„ „
9 inch/22.5 cm	„	„ 8 inch/20 cm	„	„	1½	„ „
10 inch/25 cm	„	„ 9 inch/22.5 cm	„	„	2	„ „
11 inch/27.5 cm	„	„ 10 inch/25 cm	„	„	2½	„ „
12 inch/30 cm	„	„ 11 inch/27.5 cm	„	„	3	„ „
13 inch/32.5 cm	„	„ 12 inch/30 cm	„	„	3¼	„ „

Coffee Walnut Gâteau

If there is a lot left over, then store slices in the freezer for up to 3 months.

Making time about 20 minutes
Baking time about 30–40 minutes

    6 oz/175 g (³/4 cup) soft margarine
    6 oz/175 g (1 cup) caster (very fine granulated) sugar
    3 eggs, beaten
    6 oz/175 g (1¹/2 cups) self-raising flour
    1 teaspoon baking powder
    2 oz/50 g (¹/2 cup) walnuts, chopped
    2 tablespoons coffee essence (extract)

Icing (Frosting)
    3 oz/75 g (6 tablespoons) soft margarine
    8 oz/225 g (1²/3 cups) icing (powdered) sugar, sieved
    1 tablespoon milk
    1 tablespoon coffee essence (extract)

Decoration
    about 2 oz/50 g (¹/2 cup) walnut halves

Heat the oven to 350°F, 180°C, gas mark 4. Grease and line with greased greaseproof paper two 8-inch/20-cm sandwich tins.

Measure all the ingredients for the cake into a large bowl and beat well until thoroughly blended. Divide between the prepared tins and level out evenly. Bake in the oven for about 30–40 minutes, until well risen and it springs back when lightly pressed with a finger. Leave to cool in the tins for about 5 minutes then turn out, remove paper and finish cooling on a cake rack.

For the icing, cream the margarine and icing sugar until smooth then stir in the milk and coffee essence. Sandwich the two cakes together with one-third of the icing. Spread the remainder over the top and sides of the cake and decorate with the walnut halves.

Tropical Cream Gâteau

Keep this gâteau in the refrigerator, and serve the day it is made.

Making time about 30 minutes
Baking time about 35 minutes

6 oz/175 g (³/4 cup) soft margarine
6 oz/175 g (1 cup) caster (very fine granulated) sugar
6 oz/175 g (1¹/2 cups) self-raising flour
1 teaspoon baking powder
3 eggs, beaten
grated rind of 1 orange

Icing (Frosting)
3 oz/75 g (6 tablespoons) soft margarine
8 oz/225 g (1²/3 cup) icing (powdered) sugar, sieved
2 tablespoons rum

Decoration
2 oz/50 g (²/3 cup) desiccated (shredded) coconut
1 kiwi fruit, peeled and thinly sliced
1 orange, peeled and segmented
4 glacé (candied) cherries, halved

Heat the oven to 350°F, 180°C, gas mark 4. Grease and line with greased greaseproof paper two 8-inch/20-cm round sandwich tins.

Measure all the ingredients for the cake into a large mixing bowl and beat well until thoroughly blended. Divide between the tins and level out evenly. Bake in the oven for about 35 minutes until well risen and the top of the sponges spring back when lightly pressed with a finger. Leave to cool in the tins for about 5 minutes, then turn out, remove the paper and finish cooling on a cake rack.

For the icing, measure all the ingredients into a bowl, work together then beat well until smooth. Sandwich the cakes together with one-third of the icing then spread another third over the sides and roll in the coconut. Spread the remaining icing on top of the cake and arrange the prepared fruits on top of that.

Marbled Chocolate Cake

A pretty cake which is nice to serve as a birthday cake.

Making time about 10 minutes
Baking time about 30 minutes

6 oz/175 g (1½ cups) self-raising flour
2 level teaspoons baking powder
6 oz/175 g (1 cup) caster (very fine granulated) sugar
6 oz/175 g (¾ cup) soft margarine
3 eggs, beaten
1 level tablespoon cocoa powder
1 tablespoon hot water

Icing (Frosting)
4 oz/100 g plain (semi-sweet) chocolate
3 oz/75 g (6 tablespoons) butter
4 oz/100 g (¾ cup) icing (powdered) sugar, sieved

Heat the oven to 375°F, 190°C, gas mark 5. Grease and line with greased greaseproof paper a 7 × 11-inch/17.5 × 27.5-cm deep oblong tin.

Measure all the ingredients for the cake, except the cocoa and water, into a large mixing bowl and beat well until thoroughly blended. Dot about half of this mixture in teaspoonfuls over the base of the cake tin. Mix the cocoa and water together in a bowl then mix into the remaining cake mixture until all is incorporated. Dot this over and between the plain mixture and swirl a little with a knife. Bake in the oven for about 30 minutes until well risen and the sponge springs back when lightly pressed with a finger. Leave to cool in the tin for a few moments then turn out, remove the paper and finish cooling on a cake rack.

For the icing, gently melt the chocolate and butter together in a pan then remove from the heat and stir in the icing sugar. Beat well until smooth, and spread over the top of the cake. Leave to set, then divide into about 16 squares.

Makes 16 squares

Melt-in-the-Mouth Chocolate Dessert Cake

This is a heavenly, light chocolate cake to serve with a fork. The cake itself contains no flour and has a good chocolate flavour. Do expect it to sink slightly on cooling.

Making time about 20 minutes
Baking time about 25 minutes

6 large eggs
5 oz/150 g (³/₄ cup) caster (very fine granulated) sugar
2 oz/50 g (²/₃ cup) cocoa, sieved

Filling and Topping
¹/₂ pint/300 ml (1¹/₃ cup) whipping (heavy) cream, whipped
about 8 wafer-thin mint chocolates, to decorate

Heat the oven to 350°F, 180°C, gas mark 4. Grease and line with greased greaseproof paper two 8-inch/20-cm sandwich tins.

Start by separating the eggs: put the whites in a large bowl and the yolks in a smaller bowl. Add the caster sugar and cocoa to the yolks and beat well until thick. Whisk the egg whites with an electric whisk until the mixture forms stiff peaks. Add 2 tablespoons of the whisked whites to the yolk mixture, mix thoroughly, then add this to the whites and gently fold in until thoroughly blended.

Divided between the tins and bake in the oven for about 25 minutes until just beginning to shrink back from the sides of the tins. Leave to cool in the tins for about 5 minutes then turn out, remove the paper and finish cooling on a cake rack.

When cold sandwich the two cakes together with half the cream then spread the remainder on top and decorate with the mint chocolates.

Sachertorte

This cake is dark and very rich, good to serve when somebody very special is coming to tea.

Making time about 25 minutes
Baking time about 40 minutes

4 oz/100 g (½ cup) butter, softened
5 oz/150 g (¾ cup) caster (very fine granulated) sugar
5 eggs, separated
4 oz/100 g plain (semi-sweet) chocolate, melted
1 tablespoon rum
3 oz/75 g (¾ cup) hazelnuts, chopped
3 oz/75 g (1½ cups) fresh white breadcrumbs
about 10 oz/275 g apricot jam

Icing (Frosting)
4 oz/100 g plain (semi-sweet) chocolate, broken into small pieces
3 tablespoons water
1 oz/25 g (2 tablespoons) butter
about 6 oz/175 g (1⅓ cups) icing (powdered) sugar, sieved

Heat the oven to 400°F, 200°C, gas mark 6. Grease and line with greased greaseproof paper a 9-inch/22.5-cm diameter deep round cake tin.

Put the butter, sugar, egg yolks, chocolate, rum, hazelnuts and breadcrumbs into a bowl and beat well for about 2 minutes until thoroughly blended. Whisk the egg whites in a bowl until they form stiff peaks then fold into the chocolate mixture until thoroughly blended. Turn into the prepared tin, level the top and bake in the oven for about 40 minutes until well risen and firm to the touch. Cool in the tin for about 15 minutes then turn out and remove the paper and finish cooling on a cake rack. When cool, cut into three layers and sandwich back together with the jam.

For the icing, put the chocolate, water and butter in a bowl and stand over a pan of simmering water until melted. Beat well until smooth then stir in enough icing sugar to give a coating consistency. Spread over the top and sides of the cake and allow to set before serving.

Wimbledon Cake

A really light sponge cake. Instead of strawberries, other fresh fruits such as raspberries, chopped pineapple and chopped peaches can be stirred into the cream filling.

Making time about 15 minutes
Baking time about 35 minutes

3 eggs, separated
4 oz/100 g (²/₃ cup) caster (very fine granulated) sugar
grated rind and juice of 1 small orange
3 oz/75 g (³/₄ cup) semolina

Filling
4 oz/100 g fresh strawberries, sliced
¼ pint/150 ml (²/₃ cup) whipping (heavy) cream, whipped
sieved icing (powdered) sugar to dredge on top

Heat the oven to 350°F, 180°C, gas mark 4. Grease and line with greased greaseproof paper a deep 8-inch/20-cm round cake tin.

Measure the egg yolks, sugar, grated orange rind and juice and the semolina into a bowl and beat well until thoroughly blended. In a separate bowl whisk the egg whites until they form soft peaks then gently fold them into the semolina mixture until thoroughly mixed. Turn into the prepared tin, level the top and bake in the oven for about 35 minutes until well risen and pale golden brown. The top of the cake should spring back when lightly pressed with a finger. Remove from the oven, allowed to cool in the tin for a few moments, then turn out, remove paper and finish cooling on a cake rack.

For the filling, gently stir the strawberries into the cream. Cut the cake in half horizontally and sandwich back together with the strawberries and cream. Just before serving lightly dredge with a little icing sugar.

Fresh Cream Sponge Cake

This sponge cake – topped with sprigs of mint and a few pretty flowerheads – is perfect to serve in the summer on a special occasion for tea. If you like, mix 4 oz/100 g fresh raspberries with the cream for a real treat. The sponge bases freeze well and can be frozen ahead of time then brought out of the freezer, thawed and filled when required. *See photograph facing page 49.*

Making time about 20 minutes
Baking time about 20 minutes

4 eggs
4 oz/100 g (²/₃ cup) caster (very fine granulated) sugar
4 oz/100 g (1 cup) self-raising flour

Filling
raspberry jam
¹/₂ pint/300 ml (1¹/₃ cups) whipping (heavy) cream, whipped
4 oz/100 g fresh raspberries, hulled

Decoration
a little sieved icing (powdered) sugar
a sprig of fresh mint
small flowerheads (optional)

Heat the oven to 350°F, 180°C, gas mark 4. Grease and line with greased greaseproof paper two 8-inch/20-cm sandwich tins.

Break the eggs into a warmed bowl and whisk in the sugar until the mixture is light and creamy and leaves a trail when the whisk is lifted out. Carefully fold in the flour until evenly blended. Divide the mixture between the tins and bake in the oven for about 20–30 minutes until the top of the cake springs back when lightly pressed with a finger. Turn out and leave to cool on a cake rack.

Spread both halves of the cake with raspberry jam. Sandwich the two cakes together with the whipped cream. To serve, lift on to a serving plate, dust lightly with icing sugar, and decorate with a sprig of fresh mint and a flower.

Kiwi Gâteau

The kiwi and manderins look wonderful together. Good to serve when somebody very special has come to tea. *See photograph facing page 72.*

Making time about 10 minutes
Baking time about 20 minutes

> 6 oz/175 g (¾ cup) soft margarine
> 6 oz/175 g (1½ cups) light muscovado (brown) sugar
> 3 oz/75 g (¾ cup) self-raising flour
> 3 oz/75 g (¾ cup) wholemeal (wholewheat) flour
> 1½ teaspoons baking powder
> 3 eggs, beaten
> 2 tablespoons milk

Filling and Topping
> 8 oz/225 g (1 cup) low fat soft cheese
> 1 oz/25 g icing (powdered) sugar, sieved
> grated rind of ½ lemon
> 1 kiwi fruit, peeled and sliced
> 8-oz/225-g can manderin oranges in natural juice, drained

Heat the oven to 350°F, 180°C, gas mark 4. Grease and line with greased greaseproof paper two 8-inch/20-cm sandwich tins.

Measure all the ingredients for the cake into a large mixing bowl and beat well until thoroughly blended. Divide between the prepared tins and level out evenly. Bake in the oven for about 20 minutes until the sides of the sponge have shrunk slightly from the tins and the top of the cake springs back when lightly pressed with a finger. Leave to cool in the tin for a few moments then turn out, peel off paper and finish cooling on a wire rack.

For the filling, measure the cheese, sugar and lemon rind into a bowl and beat well until blended. Reserve three slices of kiwi and six manderins for decoration then chop the remainder and stir into one-third of the filling. Sandwich the two cakes together with this mixture. Spread the remaining cheese mixture on top and decorate with the reserved kiwi and manderins.

Honey and Almond Cake

The sort of special cake that is just right for when Granny comes to tea. As this basic cake mixture is not rich, it is best to make the base on the day or day before it is needed.

Making time about 25 minutes
Baking time about 50 minutes

4 oz/100 g (½ cup) soft margarine
2 oz/50 g (½ cup) light muscovado (brown) sugar
2 level tablespoons thick honey
2 eggs
6 oz/175 g (1½ cups) self-raising flour
1 level teaspoon baking powder
4 tablespoons milk

Filling and Topping
3 oz/75 g (6 tablespoons) soft margarine
1 rounded tablespoon thick honey
3 oz/75 g (½ cup) icing (powdered) sugar, sieved
2 oz/50 g (½ cup) flaked (slivered) almonds, toasted

Heat the oven to 350°F, 180°C, gas mark 4. Grease and line with greased greaseproof paper a 7-inch/17.5-cm deep round cake tin.

Measure all the ingredients for the cake into a bowl and beat well for a minute until thoroughly blended. Turn into the prepared tin, level the top and bake in the oven for about 50 minutes until well risen. Test with a warm fine skewer: if the skewer comes out clean, then the cake is done. Leave to cool in the tin for about 10 minutes, then turn out, remove the paper and finish cooling on a cake rack.

For the filling and topping, measure the margarine, honey and sugar into a bowl and mix well until thoroughly blended. Divide the cake in half and sandwich together with half the icing. Coat the sides of the cake with half the remaining icing and roll in the toasted almonds so that the sides are evenly coated in nuts. Use the remaining icing to ice the top of the cake, then sprinkle with the remaining almonds.

Honey and Almond Swiss Roll (Jelly-Roll)

A really light and spongy Swiss roll, which is best eaten on the day it is made. *See photograph facing page 49.*

Making time about 25 minutes
Baking time 10 minutes

3 eggs
3 oz/75 g (¼ cup) thick honey
3 oz/75 g (¾ cup) wholemeal (wholewheat) flour
1 teaspoon baking powder
caster (very fine granulated) sugar

Filling
1½ oz/40 g (⅓ cup) toasted nibbed (chopped) almonds
¼ pint/150 ml (⅔ cup) whipping (heavy) cream, whipped

Heat the oven to 350°F, 180°C, gas mark 4. Grease and line a 13 × 9-inch/32.5 × 22.5-cm Swiss roll tin with greased greaseproof paper.

Break the eggs into a mixing bowl, add the honey and beat with an electric whisk or a rotary whisk for about 5 minutes until thick and the mixture leaves a trail when the whisk is lifted out. Carefully fold in the flour and baking powder until thoroughly blended. Pour into the prepared tin, spread out evenly, and bake in the oven for about 10 minutes until golden brown.

Turn the Swiss roll out on to a sheet of greaseproof paper sprinkled with caster sugar, and gently peel off the lining paper. Trim off crusty edges, cover with a piece of greaseproof paper and roll up leaving the greaseproof paper in the middle. Allow to become quite cold.

For the filling, stir the almonds into the cream. Unroll the Swiss roll, remove paper, then spread evenly with the cream. Roll it up again, and serve in slices.

Passion Fruit Sorbet (Sherbet) in Tulip Cups

These impressive cigarette russe shells are quick, but rather tricky to make. They are delicious with the passion fruit sorbet (simply divine, definitely the best flavour we have tried), but any sorbet or ice-cream can be used. Fill only at the very last minute. The mixture is baked then slipped off the baking sheet quickly and moulded to a tulip shape over a ball, a half lemon or small orange or maybe a small tall bowl.

Sorbet making time about 20 minutes
Freezing time about 8 hours
Tulip cup making and baking time about 1 hour

8 oz/225 g (1⅓ cups) caster (very fine granulated) sugar
½ pint/300 ml (1¼ cups) water
3 passion fruit
juice of 1 lemon

Tulip Cups
2 oz/50 g (¼ cup) butter
2½ oz/65 g (6 tablespoons) caster (very fine granulated) sugar
2 egg whites
2 oz/50 g (½ cup) plain (all-purpose) flour
grated rind of 1 lemon

Make the sorbet first. Put the sugar and water in a heavy based pan, heat gently and stir until sugar has dissolved. Stop stirring, bring to the boil, and boil uncovered for 5 minutes to form a light syrup. Allow to cool then cut the passion fruit in half, scoop out the middle and add the seeds and pulp with the lemon juice to the syrup.

Pour into a shallow freezer container and freeze for about 3 hours until firm around the edges and slushy in the centre. Process in a processor or mash with a fork to break down the large crystals. Return the container, seal, label and freeze until required.

To make the tulip cups, heat the oven to 425°F, 220°C, gas mark 7. Grease two baking sheets very well with lard. Cover a tennis ball with foil if using this for moulding, otherwise find a bowl to use or half a lemon.

Cream the butter and sugar together until light then beat the egg whites a little at a time until all is added. Fold in flour then spoon a teaspoonful of the mixture on to each of the sheets. Spread out with the back of a spoon to a 3-inch/7.5-cm circle. Bake no more than two at a time for about 3–4 minutes or until just tinged with brown around the edges. They have to be watched very carefully during cooking so it's best to cook one at a time to start with.

As soon as the sheets come out of the oven, lift the biscuits off with a metal spatula and mould over the tennis ball, bowl or lemon or form a cup. Leave for a few moments until firm then lift off. Repeat until all the mixture has been used.

Fill the cups at the very last minute with scoops of the sorbet.

Makes about 15 cups

Celebration Ice-Cream Cake

I often make an ice-cream cake as a birthday cake as a change from the usual sponge cake, and the children simply adore it.

Making time about 45 minutes
Freezing time about 8 hours

Raspberry Sorbet (Sherbet)
1½ lb/675 g raspberries
6 oz/175 g (1 cup) caster (very fine granulated) sugar
8 fl oz/250 ml (1 cup) water
juice of 1 large lemon

Lemon Cream Sorbet (Sherbet)
½ pint/300 ml (1⅓ cups) double (heavy) cream
grated rind and juice of 2 lemons
12 oz/350 g (2 cups) caster (very fine granulated) sugar
1 pint/600 ml (2½ cups) milk

Coating
8 oz/225 g plain (semi-sweet) chocolate, melted

For the raspberry sorbet (sherbet), reduce the raspberries to a purée in a processor or blender then sieve and discard the seeds. Measure sugar and water into a pan, heat gently until sugar has dissolved then increase the heat and boil for 5 minutes to give a light syrup. Allow to cool, then stir into the raspberry purée with the lemon juice. Turn into a 2-pint/1.2-litre (5-cup) plastic container, cover with a lid and freeze for about 8 hours until almost solid.

For the lemon cream sorbet (sherbet), put the cream in a large mixing bowl and whisk until it forms soft peaks. Stir in the remaining ingredients until thoroughly blended. Turn into a 2-pint/1.2-litre (5-cup) plastic container and freeze for about 8 hours until almost solid.

For the coating, line a 3-pint/1.75-litre (7-cup) *plastic* bowl with the melted chocolate, using the back of a spoon to spread the chocolate. Allow to set in the fridge.

When the sorbets are almost solid, cut into cubes and process each separately in a processor until thick and a spreading consistency. Alternatively use an electric whisk. Turn one into a bowl and keep in the fridge whilst processing the other, then use both to fill the chocolate mould in layers. Return to the freezer until solid. To turn out, stand the bowl in another bowl of very hot water for a few moments to loosen the chocolate from the plastic, then turn on to a serving dish, and leave at room temperature for about 5 minutes before serving.

HEALTH FOODY CAKES

Many of these cakes are made using wholemeal or wholewheat flour. Let me explain exactly what they are. These flours consist of the wholewheat grain – the outer husk or bran, the endosperm *and* the wheat germ – ground into flour. (White flours are the product of the endosperm only.) Wheatmeal flour, on the other hand, has had a percentage of the original grain extracted, thus some packets are labelled 81 or 85%, meaning that 19 or 15% of the original grain has been taken out.

These brown flours are delicious, but recipes using them will need extra raising agents as they give a close texture and the mixture will also absorb more liquid.

And, as we all know from the current ideas on nutrition, brown flours, especially the *whole* flours (wholemeal and wholewheat) are much better for us than white or wheatmeal. Both the bran and the germ are vital to health.

Banana and Carrot Cake

No one can ever guess correctly what is in this cake! It has an unusual flavour, but I think it is quite delicious and it stays nice and moist in the cake tin. You can serve it plain, or with the topping.

Making time about 10 minutes
Baking time about 1¼ hours

6 oz/175 g (¾ cup) soft margarine
6 oz/175 g (1½ cups) light muscovado (brown) sugar
3 eggs, beaten
10 oz/275 g (2½ cups) self-raising flour
2 level teaspoons baking powder
2 ripe bananas, mashed
4 oz/100 g (1 cup) carrots, grated
3 oz/75 g (¾ cup) mixed nuts (eg walnuts, hazelnuts and almonds), chopped

Topping (optional)
2 oz/50 g (¼ cup) butter, softened
2 oz/50 g (¼ cup) rich cream cheese
4 oz/100 g (¾ cup) icing (powdered) sugar, sieved
a few drops of vanilla essence (extract)

Heat the oven to 350°F, 180°C, gas mark 4, and grease and line an 8-inch/ 20-cm deep round cake tin with greased greaseproof paper.

Measure all the ingredients into a large mixing bowl and beat well for about 2 minutes until thoroughly blended. Turn into the prepared tin, level the top and bake in the oven for about 1¼ hours until well risen. Test with a warm fine skewer: if the skewer comes out clean, then the cake is done. Allow to cool in the tin for about 10 minutes, then turn out, remove paper and finish cooling on a cake rack.

If you want to use the topping, measure all the ingredients into a mixing bowl and beat well until thoroughly blended and smooth. Spread evenly over the top of the cake and rough up with a fork. Leave to harden slightly before serving.

Coffee Cake

If you have any of this cake left over then store it in the refrigerator.

Making time about 25 minutes
Baking time about 35 minutes

6 oz/175 g (³/4 cup) soft margarine
6 oz/175 g (1¹/2 cups) dark muscovado (brown) sugar
4 oz/100 g (1 cup) wholemeal (wholewheat) flour
2 oz/50 g (¹/2 cup) self-raising flour
3 level teaspoons baking powder
3 eggs
1 tablespoon coffee essence (extract)
2 tablespoons milk

Filling and Topping
1 oz/25 g (1 tablespoon) caster (very fine granulated) sugar
1 teaspoon coffee essence (extract)
2 oz/50 g (¹/2 cup) walnuts, chopped
¹/4 pint/150 ml (²/3 cup) whipping (heavy) cream, whipped

Heat the oven to 350°F, 180°C, gas mark 4. Grease and line with greased greaseproof paper two 8-inch/20-cm sandwich tins.

Measure all the ingredients for the cake into a large mixing bowl and beat well until thoroughly blended. Divide the mixture between the prepared tins, level out and bake in the oven for about 35 minutes until well risen and shrinking from the sides of the tins. Leave to cool in the tins for a minute then turn out, remove the paper and finish cooling on a cake rack.

For the filling and topping, stir the sugar, coffee essence and half the walnuts into the cream until thoroughly mixed. Use half of this cream mixture to sandwich the cakes together then spread the remainder on top and sprinkle with the remaining walnuts.

Right: Kiwi Gâteau (page 63). Photograph courtesy of the Flour Advisory Bureau.

Wholemeal Fruitcake

A good moist fruitcake which will keep well in an airtight tin. It has a close texture: for a lighter texture, use 4 oz/100 g wholemeal (wholewheat) flour and 4 oz/100 g (1 cup) self-raising flour.

Making time about 5 minutes
Baking time about 2¼ hours

2 oz/50 g (¹⁄₃ cup) glacé (candied) cherries, halved
2 oz/50 g (¹⁄₂ cup) blanched almonds, chopped
5 oz/150 g (10 tablespoons) soft margarine
5 oz/150 g (1¹⁄₄ cups) dark muscovado (brown) sugar
2 eggs, beaten
8 tablespoons milk
8 oz/225 g (2 cups) wholemeal (wholewheat) flour
2 teaspoons baking powder
10 oz/275 g (1¹⁄₃ cups) mixed dried fruit

Heat the oven to 300°F, 150°C, gas mark 2. Grease and line with greased greaseproof paper a 7-inch/17.5-cm deep round cake tin.

Measure all the ingredients into a large mixing bowl and beat well until thoroughly blended. Turn into the prepared tin, level out evenly and bake in the oven for about 2¼ hours until the cake is beginning to shrink slightly from the sides of the tin. Test with a warm fine skewer: if the skewer comes out clean, then the cake is done.

Leave to cool in the tin for about 15 minutes then turn out, remove the paper, and finish cooling on a cake rack.

Left: Rum and Raisin Cheesecake (page 84).

Walnut and Treacle Loaf

This keeps well and is always popular.

Making time 10 minutes
Baking time about 1¼ hours

4 oz/100 g (½ cup) soft margarine
3 oz/75 g (¾ cup) dark muscovado (brown) sugar
3 level tablespoons golden syrup (light corn syrup)
3 level tablespoons black treacle (molasses)
4 oz/100 g (1 cup) self-raising flour
8 oz/225 g (2 cups) wholemeal (wholewheat) flour
2 level teaspoons baking powder
3 oz/75 g (¾ cup) walnuts, chopped
scant ½ pint/300 ml (1⅓ cups) milk

Heat the oven to 325°F, 160°C, gas mark 3. Grease and line a 2-lb/900-g loaf tin with greased greaseproof paper.

Measure all the ingredients into a bowl and beat well for about 2 minutes until thoroughly blended. Turn into the prepared tin and bake in the oven for about 1¼ hours. Test with a warm fine skewer: if the skewer comes out clean, then the cake is done.

Leave to cool in the tin for about 15 minutes then turn out, remove the paper and finish cooling on a cake rack. Serve in slices.

Madeira Loaf

I don't like to use all wholemeal (wholewheat) flour but this combination with self-raising flour works very well.

Making time about 10 minutes
Baking time about 1¼ hours

8 oz/225 g (1 cup) soft margarine
6 oz/175 g (1½ cups) light muscovado (brown) sugar
6 oz/175 g (1½ cups) self-raising flour
6 oz/175 g (1½ cups) wholemeal (wholewheat) flour
2 level teaspoons baking powder
3 eggs
grated rind of 1 lemon
6 tablespoons milk

Heat the oven to 325°F, 160°C, gas mark 3. Grease and line a 2-lb/900-g loaf tin with greased greaseproof paper.

Measure all the ingredients into a large mixing bowl and beat well for about 2 minutes until thoroughly blended. Turn into the prepared tin, level the top and bake in the oven for about 1¼ hours until well risen. Test with a warm fine skewer: if the skewer comes out clean then the cake is done.

Leave to cool in the tin for about 10 minutes, then turn out, remove the paper, and finish cooling on a cake rack.

Rock Cakes

These delicious rock cakes are best eaten on the day they are made.

Making time about 10 minutes
Baking time about 15 minutes

4 oz/100 g (1 cup) self-raising flour
4 oz/100 g (1 cup) wholemeal (wholewheat) flour
3 level teaspoons baking powder
4 oz/100 g (½ cup) soft margarine
2 oz/50 g (½ cup) light muscovado (brown) sugar
6 oz/175 g (1 cup) mixed dried fruit
1 egg, beaten
1 tablespoon milk
a little demerara (brown) sugar, to sprinkle on top

Heat the oven to 400°F, 200°C, gas mark 6. Lightly grease two large baking sheets.

Measure all the ingredients into a large mixing bowl and work together until thoroughly blended to give a fairly stiff mixture. Using 2 teaspoons, spoon the mixture into 12 rough mounds on the baking sheets, sprinkle with a little demerara sugar and bake in the oven for about 15 minutes until pale golden brown at the edges. Lift off and leave to cool on a cake rack.

Makes 12 rock cakes

Coconut Slices

Ideal to include in a lunch-box or to take on a picnic.

Making time about 10 minutes
Baking time about 30 minutes

4 oz/100 g (1/2 cup) soft margarine
4 oz/100 g (1 cup) wholemeal (wholewheat) flour
2 teaspoons baking powder
4 oz/100 g (1 cup scant) sultanas (golden raisins)
2 oz/50 g (1/3 cup) raisins
1 teaspoon mixed spice (cinnamon, nutmeg, cloves, etc.)
4 oz/100 g (1 1/4 cups) desiccated (shredded) coconut
4 oz/100 g (1 cup) light muscovado (brown) sugar
2 eggs, beaten
2 tablespoons milk

Heat the oven to 350°F, 180°C, gas mark 4. Lightly grease a 7 × 11-inch/17.5 × 27.5-cm Swiss roll tin.

Measure all the ingredients into a large mixing bowl and beat well until thoroughly blended. Turn into the prepared tin and level out evenly. Bake in the oven for about 30 minutes until golden brown, and it springs back when lightly pressed with a finger.

Allow to cool in the tin and cut into 16 bars and lift out of the tin to serve.

Makes 16 bars

Chocolate Fork Biscuits

These biscuits have a really rich chocolate flavour, and keep beautifully crisp in the biscuit tin.

Making time about 10 minutes
Baking time about 12–15 minutes

    4 oz/100 g (½ cup) soft margarine
    2 oz/50 g (½ cup) light muscovado (brown) sugar
    4 oz/100 g (1 cup) wholemeal (wholewheat) flour
    1 teaspoon baking powder
    1 oz/25 g (⅓ cup) cocoa powder, sieved

Heat the oven to 375°F, 190°C, gas mark 5. Lightly grease two baking sheets.

Cream the margarine with the sugar until light then work in the flour, baking powder and cocoa until thoroughly blended and smooth. Take teaspoonfuls of the mixture and roll into balls then arrange on the baking trays. Flatten each one with a fork dipped in cold water. Bake in the oven for about 12–15 minutes.

Leave to cool on the trays for a few moments then lift off with a metal spatula and finish cooling on a cake rack.

Makes about 16 biscuits

Crunchy Shortbread Biscuits

Keep these unbaked biscuit sausages in the freezer then slice off a dozen biscuits and bake them as you need them.

Making time about 10 minutes
Baking time about 20 minutes

6 oz/175 g (³/4 cup) soft margarine
5 oz/150 g (1¹/4 cups) light muscovado (brown) sugar
4 oz/100 g (1 cup) plain (all-purpose) flour
4 oz/100 g (1 cup) wholemeal (wholewheat) flour

Heat the oven to 325°F, 160°C, gas mark 3. Lightly grease two large baking sheets.

Cream the margarine with 4 oz/100 g (1 cup) of the sugar until light, then gradually work in the flours until thoroughly blended and smooth. Divide the mixture into two and roll each into a sausage shape about 6 inches/15 cm long. Roll them in the remaining sugar, then chill in the refrigerator until firm.

Cut each sausage into 16 slices and arrange on the baking sheets. Bake in the oven for about 20 minutes or until the biscuits are pale golden brown at the edges.

Allow to cool on the trays for a few moments then lift off carefully with a metal spatula and finish cooling on a cake rack.

Makes about 32 biscuits

Fruity Flapjacks

These are really delicious! The fruit adds a bit more interest.

Making time about 5 minutes
Baking time about 35 minutes

>   *4 oz/100 g (¹/₂ cup) hard margarine*
>   *2 oz/50 g (¹/₂ cup) light muscovado (brown) sugar*
>   *2 level tablespoons golden syrup (light corn syrup)*
>   *1 level tablespoon honey*
>   *2 oz/50 g (¹/₂ cup scant) sultanas (golden raisins)*
>   *3 oz/75 g (1 cup) porridge (rolled) oats*
>   *2 oz/50 g (¹/₂ cup) wholemeal (wholewheat) flour*

Heat the oven to 325°F, 160°C, gas mark 3. Lightly grease a 7-inch/17.5-cm square tin.

Melt the margarine in a pan with the sugar, syrup and honey, then remove from the heat and stir in the sultanas, oats and flour. Mix thoroughly then turn into the tin, level out evenly and bake in the oven for about 35 minutes or until a deep golden brown.

Remove from the oven and leave to cool in the tin for about 10 minutes, then mark into 9 squares and leave in the tin to finish cooling.

Makes 9 squares

PUDDING CAKES

Pudding cakes or dessert cakes – call them what you will – are delicious at the end of a lighter meal. Serve cold ones chilled and the hot ones warm. Instead of serving all with cream, try mixing whipped cream with an equal amount of plain yoghurt, or mix cool, smooth, thickish custard with an equal quantity of single (light) cream.

Date and Apricot Cheesecake

When in season use fresh apricots, but do remember that they will need poaching for a few minutes first.

Making time about 40 minutes

1 lb/450 g fresh dates
4 oz/100 g (1/2 cup) butter, melted
8 oz/225 g (4 cups) digestive biscuits (graham crackers), crushed
1 oz/25 g (1 tablespoon) demerara (brown) sugar
15 1/2-oz/439-g can apricot halves, drained and chopped
1/2 oz/15 g (1 envelope) powdered gelatine
2 tablespoons lemon juice
2 eggs, separated
2 oz/50 g (1/3 cup) caster (very fine granulated) sugar
8 oz/225 g (1 cup) rich cream cheese

Decoration
1/4 pint/150 ml (2/3 cup) whipping (heavy) cream, whipped

Lightly grease an 8-inch/20-cm loose-bottomed cake tin.

Halve the dates lengthways, remove the stones, and arrange about half the dates in the bottom of the tin, cut side facing down. Mix together the butter, crushed biscuits and demerara, spoon over the dates and level out evenly. Spread half the chopped apricots with about another 8 dates over the biscuit mixture. Reduce the remaining apricots to a purée in a processor or blender.

Place the gelatine and lemon juice in a bowl and leave for a few minutes to form a sponge, then stand the bowl over a pan of simmering water until the gelatine has dissolved. Whisk the egg whites until stiff then add all the caster sugar a teaspoonful at a time. Beat the cream cheese with the egg yolks and stir in the gelatine. Fold in the egg whites and cream and pour into the tin.

Chill until firm. Turn out of the tin and place on a serving dish, spoon the apricot purée over the top and decorate with the remaining dates and whipped cream.

Lemon Baked Cheesecake

This is my version of the traditional baked Yorkshire cheesecake.

Making time about 15 minutes
Baking time about 40 minutes

4 oz/100 g (1 cup) plain (all-purpose) flour
2 oz/50 g (¼ cup) soft margarine
juice of ½ lemon
cold water

Filling
8 oz/225 g (1 cup) cream cheese
2 oz/50 g (½ cup) light muscovado (brown) sugar
2 eggs, beaten
grated rind and juice of 1 lemon
2 level teaspoons cornflour (cornstarch)
2 tablespoons double (heavy) cream
1 oz/25 g (2 tablespoons) butter, melted
1 oz/25 g (¼ cup) currants

Heat the oven to 425°F, 220°C, gas mark 7, and place a baking sheet in it.

For the pastry, measure the flour into a bowl and rub in the margarine until the mixture resembles fine breadcrumbs. Add the juice of the half lemon and sufficient water to form a soft dough. Turn out on to a lightly floured surface and knead until smooth. Roll out thinly and use to line a 9-inch/22.5-cm fluted flan dish. Line with a piece of greaseproof paper and weigh down with baking beans or line with a piece of foil and bake blind on the hot baking sheet for 10 minutes.

Meanwhile beat the cheese in a bowl with the sugar, eggs, rind and juice of the lemon until smooth. Blend the cornflour with the cream and stir into the mixture with the melted butter and currants. Remove the paper and beans or foil from the flan and pour in the filling. Return to the oven and reduce the temperature to 350°F, 180°C, gas mark 4 and bake for a further 30 minutes until pastry is cooked and filling has set.

Rum and Raisin Cheesecake

Once the rum and raisins have been soaked overnight, this cheesecake takes no time at all to prepare. *See photograph facing page 73.*

Making time about 20 minutes
Chilling time about 3 hours

2 oz/50 g (1/3 cup) seedless raisins, soaked overnight in 4 tablespoons rum

Crumb Crust
2 1/2 oz/65 g (5 tablespoons) butter
2 oz/50 g (1/3 cup) demerara (brown) sugar
5 oz/150 g (2 1/2 cups) digestive biscuits (graham crackers), crushed

Filling
2 eggs, separated
2 oz/50 g (1/3 cup) caster (very fine granulated) sugar
1/2 oz/15 g packet (1 envelope) powdered gelatine
3 tablespoons cold water
8 oz/225 g (1 cup) full-fat soft cheese
1/4 pint/150 ml (2/3 cup) whipping (heavy) cream

Decoration
1/4 pint/150 ml (2/3 cup) whipping (heavy) cream, whipped
raisins
chocolate curls

To make the crumb crust, melt the butter in a pan and stir in the sugar and crushed biscuits until well mixed. Press this mixture into the bottom and up the sides of a deep 9-inch/23-cm loose-bottomed flan tin. Chill in the refrigerator to harden.

For the filling, beat the egg yolks and sugar together in a bowl. Mix the gelatine with the cold water and leave to stand for 3 minutes to form a sponge. Stand the bowl of gelatine over a pan of simmering water until gelatine has completely dissolved, then remove from the heat. Allow to cool slightly then stir into the yolk

84

mixture. Whilst the gelatine is dissolving whisk the egg whites in a separate bowl until they form soft peaks. In another bowl beat the cream cheese until soft then stir in the yolk mixture. Whip the cream, and gently fold in with the egg whites and finally the soaked raisins.

Pour this mixture into the flan case and return to the refrigerator until set. Carefully lift out of the flan tin on to a serving plate and decorate with whipped cream, chocolate and raisins before serving.

Yorkshire Chocolate Flan

A very rich chocolate flan, ideal to serve after a light meal.

Making time 15–20 minutes
Chilling time about 3 hours

8 oz/225 g (1 cup) butter, softened
8 oz/225 g (1⅓ cups) caster (very fine granulated) sugar
7½ oz/200 g block plain (semi-sweet) chocolate, melted
4 tablespoons rum or brandy
1 tablespoon coffee essence (extract)
4 eggs, separated
10-inch/25-cm sponge flan (tart) case
whipping (heavy) cream, to decorate

Cream the butter and sugar in a large mixing bowl until light and creamy. Beat in the melted chocolate, half the rum or brandy, the coffee essence and egg yolks until thoroughly blended. Whisk the egg whites in a separate bowl until they form soft peaks then fold into the chocolate mixture.

Sprinkle the flan case with the remaining rum or brandy, then pour the chocolate mixture into the centre of the flan case, level the top and chill well in the refrigerator before serving, decorated with whipped cream.

Chocolate and Orange Charlotte

Use the trimmings from the sponge (lady) fingers in a trifle or crumbled over a fruit fool or yoghurt.

Making time about 20 minutes
Chilling time about 2 hours

1 packet 16 sponge (lady) fingers
4 oz/100 g (½ cup) butter, softened
4 oz/100 g (⅔ cup) caster (very fine granulated) sugar
2 eggs, separated
4 oz/100 g plain (semi-sweet) chocolate, melted
finely grated rind and juice of 1 orange

To decorate
¼ pint/150 ml (⅔ cup) whipping (heavy) cream, whipped
1 packet chocolate buttons (drops)

Trim the rounded ends off each sponge finger and use to cover the base of a loose-bottomed 7-inch/17.5-cm square tin, arranging the fingers with the sugared side facing downwards.

Beat together the butter, sugar and egg yolks in a large mixing bowl until soft and smooth, then stir in the melted chocolate and orange rind and juice.

Whisk the egg whites in a separate bowl until they form soft peaks then fold into the chocolate mixture. Pour into the prepared tin, level the top and leave in the refrigerator for about 2 hours to set.

To serve, turn out on to a serving dish, pipe swirls of cream on top of the cake and decorate each swirl with a chocolate button.

Butterscotch Refrigerator Cake

This cake needs about 4 hours in the refrigerator to set, and it's rather fattening – so only serve in thin slices!

Making time about 15 minutes
Chilling time about 4 hours

6 oz/175 g (³/₄ cup) unsalted butter
4 good tablespoons golden syrup (light corn syrup)
4 oz/100 g (²/₃ cup) glacé (candied) cherries, chopped
4 oz/100 g (²/₃ cup) dates, chopped
4 oz/100 g (³/₄ cup) seedless raisins, roughly chopped
4 oz/100 g (1 cup) walnuts, roughly chopped
8 oz/225 g (4 cups) digestive biscuits (graham crackers), crumbled
a little whipped cream, to serve

Measure the butter and golden syrup into a heavy pan, heat gently until butter has melted, then increase heat and boil for about 3 minutes, stirring all the time. Leave on one side to cool.

Place all the remaining ingredients, except for the cream, in a large bowl, pour over the cooled sauce and mix well until evenly coated. Turn the mixture into an 8-inch/20-cm loose-bottomed cake tin and leave in the refrigerator for at least 4 hours to set before serving.

When set, turn out, cut into thin slices and serve with a swirl of cream on top.

Cuts into about 10 slices

Strawberry Pavlova

Make this recipe several hours before you plan to serve it as it improves if allowed to stand in the fridge for a while.

Making time about 15 minutes
Baking time about 1 hour

Pavlova
  3 large egg whites
  6 oz/175 g (1 cup) caster (very fine granulated) sugar
  ½ teaspoon white wine vinegar
  2 level teaspoons cornflour (cornstarch)

Filling
  1 lb/450 g strawberries
  ½ pint/300 ml (1⅓ cups) whipping (heavy) cream, whipped

Heat the oven to 275°F, 140°C, gas mark 1. Lay a sheet of silicone paper on a baking sheet and mark an 8-inch/20-cm circle on it.

Whisk the egg whites until stiff, whisk in the sugar a teaspoonful at a time, adding the vinegar and cornflour to the meringue with the last spoon of sugar. Spread the meringue on the silicone paper to cover the circle, building up the sides to come higher than the centre. Bake in the oven for about an hour, then turn off the oven and leave the meringue to cool in the oven. When cold lift the meringue on to a serving plate.

Reduce half the strawberries to a purée in a processor or blender and stir into the whipped cream. Pile this on to the centre of the meringue and decorate with the remaining strawberries. Leave to stand in the refrigerator for at least an hour before serving.

Raspberry Shortcake

Always a great favourite, this tastes just as good filled with strawberries.

Making time about 20 minutes
Baking time about 20 minutes

6 oz/175 g (1½ cups) self-raising flour
4 oz/100 g (½ cup) butter
3 oz/75 g (½ cup) caster (very fine granulated) sugar
half an egg, beaten
6 oz/175 g raspberries
¼ pint/150 ml (⅔ cup) whipping (heavy) cream, whipped
a little icing (powdered) sugar, to dust on top

Heat the oven to 375°F, 190°C, gas mark 5. Lightly grease a large baking sheet.

Measure the flour into a bowl and rub in the butter until the mixture resembles fine breadcrumbs. Add the sugar and beaten egg and knead together. Turn out on to a lightly floured surface and knead until smooth. Divide in half and roll out each piece to an 8-inch/20-cm round, lift on to the prepared baking sheet and bake in the oven for about 20 minutes until pale golden brown. Allow to cool on the sheet for a few moments then carefully lift off and finish cooling on cake racks.

For the filling, mix the raspberries into the cream, saving a few for decoration, then pile on top of one of the pieces of shortcake. Lift the other piece of shortcake on top, dust with a little icing sugar, and decorate with the reserved raspberries.

Coffee Ring

This sponge ring is lovely and light. Be sure to grease the ring mould very well otherwise it may stick.

Making time about 15 minutes
Baking time about 35 minutes

> *3 eggs*
> *3 oz/75 g (1/2 cup) caster (very fine granulated) sugar*
> *3 oz/75 g (3/4 cup) self-raising flour*
> *3 tablespoons sunflower oil*
> *3 tablespoons coffee essence (extract)*

Topping
> *4 oz/100 g (3/4 cup) icing (powdered) sugar, sieved*
> *1 tablespoon coffee essence (extract)*
> *a little cold water*

Heat the oven to 350°F, 180°C, gas mark 4. Grease a 2-pint/1.2-litre (5-cup) metal ring mould really well with melted lard.

Break the eggs into a large mixing bowl, add the sugar and whisk with an electric whisk until the mixture leaves a trail when the whisk is lifted out. Carefully fold the flour into the mixture with the oil and coffee essence until thoroughly blended then gently turn into the prepared ring mould. Level out evenly and bake in the oven for about 35 minutes until the cake is beginning to shrink away from the sides of the mould. Allow to cool in the ring mould for a few moments then loosen the edges carefully with a knife and turn out on to a cake rack to finish cooling.

For the topping, measure the icing sugar into a bowl, add the coffee essence and sufficient water to give a smooth icing. When the cake is cold pour the icing over the ring so that it just begins to run down the sides of the ring. Lift on to a serving plate to serve.

Coconut Cake

A good coconut cake which is delicious served warm as a pudding.

Making time 10 minutes
Baking time about 1 hour

4 eggs
8 oz/225 g (1¹/₃ cups) caster (very fine granulated) sugar
2 oz/50 g (¹/₂ cup) self-raising flour
¹/₂ teaspoon baking powder
1 teaspoon vanilla essence (extract)
scant 1 pint/550-600 ml (2¹/₂ cups) milk
3 oz/75 g (1 cup) desiccated (shredded) coconut
2 oz/50 g (¹/₄ cup) soft margarine

Heat the oven to 350°F, 180°C, gas mark 4. Lightly butter a 10-inch/25-cm ovenproof round dish.

Measure all the ingredients into a large mixing bowl and beat well until thoroughly blended. Pour into the prepared dish and bake in the oven for about an hour until golden brown.

Gooseberry Sponge Pudding

Serve this sponge hot with ice-cream or custard. Blackcurrants also go well in this recipe.

Making time about 15 minutes
Baking time about 1 hour

1lb/450 g gooseberries, topped and tailed
3 oz/75 g (1/2 cup) granulated sugar
4 oz/100 g (1/2 cup) soft margarine
4 oz/100 g (1 cup) light muscovado (brown) sugar
2 eggs, beaten
2 oz/50 g (1/2 cup) self-raising flour
2 oz/50 g (1/2 cup) wholemeal (wholewheat) flour
1 good teaspoon baking powder
a few flaked (slivered) almonds, to sprinkle on top

Heat the oven to 350°F, 180°C, gas mark 4. Lightly butter a 2-pint/1.2-litre (5-cup) ovenproof dish, and put in the gooseberries and the granulated sugar. Place in the oven whilst preparing the sponge.

Put the margarine, muscovado sugar, eggs, flours and baking powder in a bowl and beat well until thoroughly blended. Remove the dish from the oven and spread the sponge mixture over the gooseberries. Spinkle with almonds and return to the oven. Bake for about an hour until the cake is a golden brown, and springs back when lightly pressed with a finger. Serve straightaway.

Serves 6

Eve's Pudding

Make this at the same time as making a Victoria sandwich cake as it uses the same mixture.

Making time about 10 minutes
Baking time about 1 hour

> 1 lb/450 g Bramley (tart) apples, peeled and cored and sliced
> 3 oz/75 g (¾ cup) light muscovado (brown) sugar
> grated rind and juice of 1 lemon
> 4 oz/100 g (½ cup) soft margarine
> 4 oz/100 g (⅔ cup) caster (very fine granulated) sugar
> 2 eggs, beaten
> 4 oz/100 g (1 cup) self-raising flour
> 1 teaspoon baking powder

Heat the oven to 350°F, 180°C, gas mark 4. Grease a 2-pint/1.2-litre (5-cup) ovenproof dish and arrange the apples in the bottom with the muscovado sugar, lemon rind and juice.

Measure the remaining ingredients into a large mixing bowl and beat well until thoroughly blended. Spread the mixture over the apples and bake in the oven for about 1 hour until the apple is tender and the sponge springs back when lightly pressed with a finger.

Serves 6

Apple and Lemon Pudding Cake

A lovely light pudding. Serve straight from the oven with cream.

Making time about 10 minutes
Baking time about 50 minutes

4 large Bramley (tart) apples
grated rind and juice of 1 lemon
2½ oz/65 g (1¼ cups) fresh soft brown breadcrumbs
1 tablespoon butter, melted
caster (very fine granulated) sugar
2 eggs, separated

Heat the oven to 350°F, 180°C, gas mark 4. Generously butter a 2½-pint/ 1.4-litre (6-cup) ovenproof dish.

Peel and coarsely grate the apples into a large bowl, stir in the lemon rind and juice, breadcrumbs, melted butter, 3 oz/75 g (½ cup) caster sugar and the egg yolks and mix thoroughly.

In another bowl whisk the egg whites until stiff. Whisk in 3 tablespoons caster sugar, a teaspoonful at a time, and whisk well after each addition. Whisk the meringue into the apple mixture, turn at once into the prepared dish and bake in the oven for about 50 minutes until pale golden brown and crisp on top. Serve straightaway.

Serves 6

Bramley Apple Cake

A delicious cake to serve warm as a pudding.

Making time about 20 minutes
Baking time about 1 hour 20 minutes

8 oz/225 g (2 cups) self-raising flour
1 level teaspoon baking powder
grated rind of 1 lemon
½ teaspoon mixed spice (cinnamon, cloves, nutmeg, etc.)
4 oz/100 g (1 cup) light muscovado (brown) sugar
4 oz/100 g (⅔ cup) sultanas (golden raisins)
4 oz/100 g (½ cup) soft margarine
1 egg, beaten
4 tablespoons milk
1 lb/450 g Bramley (tart) apples, peeled, cored and chopped

Topping
1 tablespoon demerara (brown) sugar

Heat the oven to 350°F, 180°C, gas mark 4. Lightly grease an 8-inch/20-cm loose-bottomed round cake tin.

Measure all the ingredients into a large bowl and work together until thoroughly blended. Turn into the prepared tin. Level the top and bake in the oven for about 1 hour 20 minutes until golden brown and shrinking slightly from the sides of the tin.

Cool for a few moments in the tin, then turn out. Sprinkle the demerara sugar on top and serve warm with cream.

Right: Good Almond Slices (page 112), Coffee and Chocolate Eclairs (pages 120–121) and Lemon Cream Strawberry Tarts (page 117).

Apple Puffas

Phyllo pastry is available from all good delicatessens and Greek shops. It needs to be handled with great care as the sheets of pastry are very thin.

Making time about 20 minutes
Baking time about 20 minutes

Filling
  2 medium cooking (tart) apples, peeled, cored and chopped
  ½ teaspoon ground cinnamon
  2 oz/50 g (⅓ cup) demerara (brown) sugar
  2 oz/50 g (¼ cup) butter

For the pastry
  1-lb/450-g packet phyllo pastry
  6 oz/175 g (¾ cup) butter, melted

Heat the oven to 400°F, 200°C, gas mark 6. Lightly grease two baking sheets.

Start by preparing the filling. Gently cook the apple, cinnamon, sugar and butter in a small pan until the apple is just tender. Allow to cool.

To assemble the puffas, carefully unroll the phyllo pastry. Take two sheets of the pastry and brush over evenly with melted butter, lay one on top of the other and divide in half lengthwise. Spoon a generous blob of the apple filling on to one corner of the strips of pastry and fold this corner over to form a triangle. Keep folding the triangle over until you reach the end of the strip of pastry and the filling is secured inside a triangle of pastry. Repeat this until all the sheets of pastry and apple filling have been used. Arrange on the baking sheets, brush with more melted butter and bake in the oven for about 20 minutes until crisp and golden brown. Serve warm with cream.

Serves 6–8

Left: Abbey Biscuits (page 141), Chocolate Shortbread Fingers (page 136) and Florentines (page 130).

Gingered Apple Roll

Swiss roll is delicious filled with any stewed fruit, and you can try this recipe with blackberry and apple instead of the apple and ginger in the autumn when the brambles are laden with blackberries.

Making time about 15 minutes
Baking time about 10 minutes

>   *3 eggs*
>   *3 oz/75 g (¹/₂ cup) caster (very fine granulated) sugar*
>   *3 oz/75 g (³/₄ cup) self-raising flour*
>   *1 teaspoon ground ginger*

Filling
>   *2 medium cooking (tart) apples, peeled, cored and chopped*
>   *2 tablespoons demerara (brown) sugar*
>   *1 oz/25 g (2 tablespoons) butter*
>   *1 oz/25 g stem (preserved) ginger, drained and chopped*
>   *caster (very fine granulated) sugar to sprinkle on top*

Heat the oven to 425°F, 220°C, gas mark 7. Grease and line with greased greaseproof paper a 9 × 13-inch/2.5 × 32.5-cm Swiss roll tin.

Break the eggs into a large bowl, add the sugar, and whisk with a rotary or electric whisk until the mixture leaves a trail when the whisk is lifted out. Fold in the flour and ground ginger until thoroughly mixed then turn into the prepared tin. Level out evenly and bake in the oven for about 10 minutes until golden brown and beginning to shrink away from the sides of the tin.

Meanwhile prepare the filling. Cook the apple, sugar, butter and stem ginger in a pan over a low heat until the apple is just tender, stirring occasionally.

While the cake finishes cooking, cut a piece of greaseproof paper a little bigger than the tin and sprinkle with caster sugar. Invert the cake on to the sugared paper. Carefully loosen and peel off the paper from the bottom of the sponge. To make rolling easier, trim all four edges of the sponge and make a score mark

1-inch/2.5-cm in from the end nearest you, being careful not to cut right through. Spread the sponge with the stewed apple, taking it almost to the edges. Fold the narrow strip created by the score mark down on to the apple and begin rolling, using the paper to help keep a firm roll.

Leave for a few minutes with the paper still around it so that it will settle. Allow to cool, then remove the paper, and lift on to a serving plate. Sprinkle with a little more caster sugar just before serving.

Serves 6

Meringue Cake

Serve this cake as a pudding when you have a hungry family to feed.

Making time about 20 minutes
Baking time about 35 minutes

    6 oz/175 g (³/4 cup) soft margarine
    6 oz/175 g (1¹/3 cups) caster (very fine granulated) sugar
    3 eggs, beaten
    6 oz/175 g (1¹/2 cups) self-raising flour
    1 teaspoon baking powder

Filling
    about 3 tablespoons apricot jam

Topping
    1 egg white
    2 oz/50 g (¹/3 cup) caster (very fine granulated) sugar
    2 oz/50 g (¹/2 cup) toasted flaked (slivered) almonds

Heat the oven to 350°F, 180°C, gas mark 4. Grease and line with greased greaseproof paper two 8-inch/20-cm round sandwich tins.

Measure all the ingredients for the cake into a large bowl and beat well until thoroughly blended. Divide between the prepared tins and level out evenly. Bake in the oven for about 35 minutes until pale golden brown and the top of the sponge springs back when lightly pressed with a finger. Leave to cool in the tin for a few minutes then turn out and finish cooling on a cake rack. When cold sandwich the sponges together with the jam.

For the topping, preheat the grill (broiler) to very hot. Whisk the egg white until it forms stiff peaks then add the sugar a teaspoonful at a time, whisking well after each addition until all the sugar has been added. Spread the meringue over the top of the cake, rough up with a fork and sprinkle with the almonds. Place under the hot grill for about 3 minutes until the meringue is tinged with golden brown. Serve straightaway.

TARTS AND PASTRIES

Although I have usually suggested making your own pastry you could, of course, use frozen pastry, either shortcrust (basic) or puff. I often make shortcrust pastry to the rubbed fat into the flour stage, then store it in the fridge; all that I need to add thereafter is water for pastry, or some sugar for fruit crumbles.

Strawberry Shortcakes

This recipe makes me think of summer and hot sunny afternoons!

Making time about 15 minutes
Baking time about 10 minutes

8 oz/225 g (2 cups) self-raising flour
3 oz/75 g (6 tablespoons) soft margarine
1 oz/25 g (1 tablespoon) caster (very fine granulated) sugar
1 egg, beaten
about 4 tablespoons milk
a little milk to glaze

Filling
¼ pint/150 ml (²/₃ cup) whipping (heavy) cream, whipped
8 oz/225 g strawberries, sliced
a little icing (powdered) sugar, sieved to dust

Heat the oven to 425°F, 220°C, gas mark 7. Lightly grease a large baking sheet.

Measure the flour into a bowl and rub in the margarine until the mixture resembles fine breadcrumbs. Stir in the sugar and mix to a soft dough with the egg and milk. Turn out on to a lightly floured surface and knead until smooth then roll out to ½-inch/12-mm thickness and cut into 6 rounds with a plain 3½-inch/9-cm cutter. Arrange on the baking sheet. Glaze with a little milk and bake in the oven for about 10 minutes until well risen and golden brown. Lift on to a cake rack to cool.

To serve, slice the shortcakes in half and sandwich together with the cream and strawberries. Arrange on a serving plate and dust with a little icing sugar.

Apple and Mincemeat Slices

I often make these at Christmas time, as they are less time-consuming than making individual pies. They're best eaten on the day they are made.

Making time about 20 minutes
Baking time about 30 minutes

10 oz/275 g (2½ cups) plain (all-purpose) flour
6 oz/175 g (¾ cup) soft margarine
1 oz/25 g (1 tablespoon) caster (very fine granulated) sugar
1 egg, beaten

Filling
2 oz/50 g (½ cup) light muscovado (brown) sugar
4 rounded tablespoons mincemeat
juice of ½ lemon
1 large Bramley (tart) apple, peeled, cored and sliced
a little icing (powdered) sugar

Heat the oven to 400°F, 200°C, gas mark 6. Lightly grease a 7 × 11-inch/17.5 × 27.5-cm Swiss roll tin.

Measure the flour into a bowl, and rub in the margarine until the mixture resembles fine breadcrumbs. Stir in the sugar and bind together with the egg to give a firm dough. Turn out on to a lightly floured surface and knead gently until smooth. Divide dough into two. Wrap one half in clingfilm and chill in the refrigerator for a few minutes. Press the other half into the bottom of the tin.

For the filling, measure all the ingredients into a bowl and mix well. Spread over the top of the pastry in the tin. Roll out the remaining chilled pastry to fit the tin and carefully lift on top of the mincemeat mixture using the rolling pin for support. Press down the sides to seal the edges.

Bake in the oven for about 30 minutes until pale golden brown. Dredge with a little icing sugar and leave to cool in the tin before cutting into 16 fingers and lifting out with a metal spatula.

Makes 16 fingers

Mincemeat and Meringue Tarts

These tarts are best served warm and when freshly made.

Making time 25 minutes
Baking time about 30 minutes

6 oz/175 g (1½ cups) plain (all-purpose) flour
1½ oz/40 g (3 tablespoons) margarine
1½ oz/40 g (3 tablespoons) lard
about 2 tablespoons water

Filling
mincemeat

Topping
2 egg whites
4 oz/100 g (⅔ cup) caster (very fine granulated) sugar

Heat the oven to 375°F, 190°C, gas mark 5.

For the pastry, measure the flour into a bowl and rub in the fats until the mixture resembles fine breadcrumbs. Add sufficient water to give a firm dough then turn out on to a lightly floured surface and knead until smooth. Roll out thinly and cut out 12 circles to line deep bun tins. Fill each tart with a teaspoon of mincemeat. Be sure not to overfill the tarts as the mincemeat may boil out. Bake in the oven for about 20 minutes until the pastry is cooked.

For the topping, whisk the egg whites with an electric whisk until they form soft peaks then whisk in the sugar a teaspoonful at a time, whisking well after each addition to give a firm meringue. Spoon the meringue on top of the tarts so that the mincemeat is sealed inside. Return to the oven for about 10 minutes until the meringue is beginning to tinge with golden brown. Cool in the bun tin.

Makes 12

Mincemeat
Bakewell Tart

Serve either warm or cold. A rather different way of serving this traditional tart, the mincemeat complements the almond flavour well.

Making time about 20 minutes
Baking time about 30 minutes

6 oz/175 g (1½ cups) plain (all-purpose) flour
1½ oz/40 g (3 tablespoons) lard
1½ oz/40 g (3 tablespoons) margarine
about 2 tablespoons water

Filling
4 oz/100 g (½ cup) butter
4 oz/100 g (⅔ cup) caster (very fine granulated) sugar
1 egg, beaten
4 oz/100 g (1 cup) semolina
½ teaspoon almond essence (extract)
2 good tablespoons mincemeat

Heat the oven to 400°F, 200°C, gas mark 6.

Measure the flour into a bowl and rub in the fats until the mixture resembles fine breadcrumbs. Add sufficient water to mix to a firm dough. Roll out thinly on a lightly floured surface and line an 8-inch/20-cm loose-bottomed flan tin. Prick the base with a fork and chill in the refrigerator whilst preparing the filling.

Heat the butter in a small pan until it has just melted, stir in sugar, beaten egg, semolina and almond essence.

Spread the mincemeat over the base of the pastry case and spread the buttery filling on top. Bake in the oven for about 30 minutes until golden brown, and the filling springs back when lightly pressed with a finger. Leave to cool on a cake rack then lift out of the tin and serve in slices.

Serves 6

Pear and Mincemeat Pastie

Best served warm. If you have a glut of either pears or apples in the garden this is a good way of using them up.

Making time about 10 minutes
Baking time about 40 minutes

14 oz/397 g packet frozen puff pastry, thawed
8 oz/225 g (1 cup) mincemeat
2–3 pears
a little demerara (brown) sugar

Heat the oven to 425°F, 220°C, gas mark 7.

Roll out the pastry on a lightly floured surface to an oblong 24 × 9 inches/ 60 × 22.5 cm, and cut across in half. Take one piece of the pastry, fold in half and cut 2-inch/5-cm slits along the folded edge. Open it out again.

Place the plain piece of pastry on a baking sheet and spread the mincemeat over it, leaving 1 inch/2.5 cm around the border. Peel, core and slice the pears and arrange on top of the mincemeat. Wet the edges of the pastry with water and cover with the cut piece of pastry. Seal the edges together, brush the surface with cold water and sprinkle with demerara sugar. Bake in the oven for about 40 minutes until the pastry is golden brown and the pears are tender. Serve in slices.

Serves 6

Macaroon Mincemeat Tarts

Eat on the day they are prepared. For an extra strong almond flavour, add a few drops of almond essence (extract).

Making time about 20 minutes
Baking time about 30 minutes

6 oz/175 g (1½ cups) plain (all-purpose) flour
1½ oz/40 g (3 tablespoons) margarine
1½ oz/40 g (3 tablespoons) lard
about 2 tablespoons water

Filling
mincemeat

Topping
3 egg whites
4 oz/100 g (⅔ cups) caster (very fine granulated) sugar
4 oz/100 g (1 cup) ground almonds
a few flaked (slivered) almonds to sprinkle on top

Heat the oven to 375°F, 190°C, gas mark 5.

Measure the flour into a bowl, rub in the fats until the mixture resembles fine breadcrumbs, then add sufficient water to give a firm dough. Turn out on to a lightly floured surface and knead until smooth. Roll out thinly and cut out circles with a fluted pastry cutter. Use to line 12 patty tins, and spread a little mincemeat in the bottom of each tart.

For the topping, whisk the egg whites until stiff then whisk in the sugar a teaspoonful at a time until all the sugar has been added. Fold in the almonds then divide between the tarts, sealing the mincemeat in the middle. Sprinkle each tart with a few flaked almonds then bake in the oven for about 30 minutes until the topping is golden brown and the pastry is cooked.

Makes 12 tarts

Lemon, Syrup and Apple Tart

An extra special treacle tart. Delicious served warm.

Making time 15 minutes
Baking time 45 minutes

6 oz/175 g (1½ cups) plain (all-purpose) flour
1½ oz/40 g (3 tablespoons) lard
1½ oz/40 g (3 tablespoons) margarine
about 2 tablespoons water

Filling
1 cooking (tart) apple (about 8 oz/225 g before peeling), peeled, cored and diced
grated rind and juice of 1 lemon
2 eggs, beaten
2 oz/50 g (1 cup) fresh white breadcrumbs
6 fl oz/175 ml (6 tablespoons) golden syrup (light corn syrup)
¼ pint/150 ml (⅔ cup) double (heavy) cream

Heat the oven to 375°F, 190°C, gas mark 5. Put a baking sheet in the oven to heat through.

Measure the flour into a bowl, rub in the fats until the mixture resembles fine breadcrumbs, then mix to a firm dough with the water. Turn out on to a lightly floured surface, knead until smooth, then roll out and use to line a 9-inch/ 22.5-cm loose-bottomed flan tin. Chill in the refrigerator whilst preparing the filling.

For the filling, mix all the ingredients together until thoroughly blended then pour into the flan tin. Bake in the oven on the baking sheet for about 45 minutes until the filling has set and the pastry is cooked.

Serve 6–8

Cherry and Lemon Tart

If preferred, you could use a biscuit crust base instead of the pastry – digestive biscuits (graham crackers), butter and sugar.

Making time about 20 minutes
Baking time about 30 minutes

> *5 oz/150 g (10 tablespoons) margarine*
> *3 oz/75 g (1/2 cup) caster (very fine granulated) sugar*
> *8 oz/225 g (2 cups) plain (all-purpose) flour*

Filling
> *juice and rind of 1 lemon*
> *6.91-oz/196-g can condensed milk*
> *1/4 pint/150 ml (2/3 cup) double (heavy) cream*
> *14-oz/400-g can cherry pie filling*

Heat the oven to 325°F, 160°C, gas mark 3.

Melt the margarine gently in the large saucepan, add the sugar and heat until the sugar has dissolved. Remove from the heat and gradually add the flour. Work it in until it is all evenly blended and smooth.

While it is still warm, press the dough and mould it into the shape of a 10-inch/ 25-cm shallow loose-bottomed flan tin with the back of a metal spoon or your hand. Bring it up a little at the edges so that it will shrink back to the correct height as it is baked. Prick the base all over with a fork then bake in the oven for about 30 minutes. If the edges brown after a little while, cover them with foil and continue cooking until the base is lightly browned as well. Leave flan to cool then lift out on to a flat plate.

To make the filling, whisk the lemon rind and juice, condensed milk and cream in a large bowl until the mixture starts to thicken. Pour this into the cooled pastry case and leave in the refrigerator to set. When the lemon filling is set, gently spread the pie filling over the top to cover it completely. Serve the tart chilled.

Serves 8

Treacle Tart

Treacle tart is one of those favourites that is so easy to prepare and always has the family coming back for second helpings. I try to keep breadcrumbs in the freezer so that they are easily at hand for recipes such as this.

Making time about 15 minutes
Baking time about 30–35 minutes

6 oz/175 g (1½ cups) plain (all-purpose) flour
1½ oz/40 g (3 tablespoons) lard
1½ oz/40 g (3 tablespoons) margarine
about 2 tablespoons cold water

Filling
about 9 good tablespoons golden syrup (light corn syrup)
about 5 oz/150 g (2½ cups) fresh white or brown breadcrumbs
grated rind and juice of 1 large lemon

Heat the oven to 400°F, 200°C, gas mark 6.

Measure the flour into a bowl and rub in the fats until the mixture resembles fine breadcrumbs. Add sufficient water to mix to a firm dough. Roll out thinly on a lightly floured surface and use to line a 9-inch/22.5-cm loose-bottomed flan tin.

Heat the syrup in a large pan until runny and stir in the breadcrumbs, lemon rind and juice. (It may be necessary to add a few more breadcrumbs if the mixture looks too runny.) Turn into the pastry case and level out evenly. Bake in the oven for 10 minutes, then reduce the oven temperature to 350°F, 180°C, gas mark 4 and bake for a further 20–25 minutes until the tart is cooked. Leave to cool in the tin then lift out and serve in wedges.

Serves 8

Apple and Almond Flan

Serve warm with whipped cream. It's also very good, wrapped carefully, taken on a picnic to serve cold.

Making time 20 minutes
Baking time about 40 minutes

> 4 oz/100 g (1 cup) plain (all-purpose) flour
> 1½ oz/40 g (3 tablespoons) butter
> 1½ oz/40 g (3 tablespoons) lard
> ½ oz/15 g (2 teaspoons) caster (very fine granulated) sugar
> 1 egg yolk

Filling
> 2 oz/50 g (⅓ cup) currants
> 1 oz/25 g (¼ cup) ground almonds
> 2 oz/50 g (⅓ cup) demerara (brown) sugar
> 1½ lb/675 g Bramley (tart) apples, peeled, cored and sliced
> 4 tablespoons apricot jam
> 2 tablespoons water

Heat the oven to 400°F, 200°C, gas mark 6.

Measure the flour into a bowl and rub in the fats until the mixture resembles fine breadcrumbs. Stir in the sugar then bind to a firm dough with the egg yolk. Roll out thinly on a lightly floured surface and use to line an 8-inch/20-cm loose-bottomed flan tin. Chill in the refrigerator whilst preparing the filling.

Mix the currants, ground almonds and sugar in a bowl. Arrange half the apple slices in the bottom of the pastry-lined flan tin then spread the currant mixture on top. Add a final layer of the remaining apple, arranged neatly, on top. Measure the jam and water into a pan and heat gently until the jam has melted. Sieve, then brush a thin layer over the top of the apples. Reserve the rest for later. Bake in the oven for about 40 minutes until the pastry is golden brown and the apples are tender. Warm the reserved jam through again and spoon evenly over the apples. Serve in wedges.

Serves 6

Good Almond Slices

I often make this recipe to give as a present for Mothering Sunday or for aunts' birthdays or thank-you presents. It is always appreciated as much as a bunch of flowers. They can be made in a Swiss roll tin or a flan tin. *See photograph facing page 96.*

Making time about 20 minutes
Baking time about 30 minutes

> *6 oz/175 g (1½ cups) plain (all-purpose) flour*
> *1½ oz/40 g (3 tablespoons) margarine*
> *1½ oz/40 g (3 tablespoons) lard*
> *about 2 tablespoons cold water*

Filling
> *4 oz/100 g (½ cup) butter*
> *4 oz/100 g (⅔ cup) caster (very fine granulated) sugar*
> *1 egg, beaten*
> *4 oz/100 g (1 cup) semolina*
> *a few drops of almond essence*
> *3 tablespoons raspberry jam*
> *a few flaked (slivered) almonds*

Heat the oven to 400°F, 200°C, gas mark 6.

For the pastry, measure the flour into a bowl and rub in the fats until the mixture resembles fine breadcrumbs. Add sufficient water to mix to a firm dough, then knead until smooth. Roll out the pastry on a lightly floured surface and use to line a 7 × 11-inch/17.5 × 27.5-cm Swiss roll tin. Prick the base with a fork and chill in the refrigerator.

For the filling, melt the butter in a pan then remove from the heat and stir in the sugar, egg, semolina and almond essence. Beat well. Spread the jam over the pastry then pour over the filling and level out evenly. Sprinkle with flaked almonds and bake in the oven for about 30 minutes until golden brown and the pastry is cooked. Leave to cool completely in the tin, then mark into 12 slices.

Makes 12 slices

Banana Tarts

I cheat with this recipe, and buy the pastry cases already made.

Making time about 10 minutes

16 small bought pastry cases

Filling
¼ pint/150 ml (⅔ cup) whipping (heavy) cream
2 bananas
3 oz/75 g plain (semi-sweet) chocolate

Whisk the cream until it is thick and divide between the pastry cases. Slice the bananas and arrange 3 slices on top of each tart on top of the cream.

Break the chocolate into pieces, place in a bowl and stand the bowl over a pan of simmering water until the chocolate has melted and is smooth.

Make a small piping bag with greaseproof paper and snip off the tip. Fill with the melted chocolate and pipe a trail of chocolate backwards and forwards over each tart. Leave to set before serving.

Makes 16 tarts

Cheesecake Tartlets

Serve these straight from the oven as a pudding.

Making time about 20 minutes
Baking time about 25 minutes

4 oz/100 g (1 cup) plain (all-purpose) flour
2 oz/50 g (¼ cup) soft margarine
½ oz/15 g (2 teaspoons) caster (very fine granulated) sugar
about 2 teaspoons cold water
1 egg yolk

Filling
1 egg
2 oz/50 g (⅓ cup) caster (very fine granulated) sugar
2 level teaspoons plain (all-purpose) flour
4 oz/100 g (½ cup) cream cheese
8 oz/225 g canned apricots, well drained and roughly chopped

Heat the oven to 375°F, 190°C, gas mark 5.

Measure the flour into a bowl and rub in the margarine until the mixture resembles fine breadcrumbs. Stir in the sugar and mix to a firm dough with the water and egg yolk. Turn out on to a lightly floured surface and knead until smooth then roll out thinly and use to line 12 patty tin or individual tart tins.

For the filling, blend the egg, sugar and flour together then beat in the cream cheese and chopped apricots. Divide the mixture between the tarts and bake in the oven for about 25 minutes until the pastry is cooked and the filling has set.

Makes 12 tartlets

Marmalade Surprise Cakes

If liked then these small cakes can be iced with a little orange glacé icing (basic glaze).

Making time about 20 minutes
Baking time about 35 minutes

8 oz/225 g (2 cups) plain (all-purpose) flour
2 oz/50 g (¼ cup) margarine
2 oz/50 g (¼ cup) lard
about 8 teaspoons water

Filling
about 5 tablespoons orange marmalade

Topping
4 oz/100 g (½ cup) soft margarine
4 oz/100 g (⅔ cup) caster (very fine granulated) sugar
2 eggs
4 oz/100 g (1 cup) self-raising flour
1 teaspoon baking powder
grated rind of 1 orange

Heat the oven to 350°F, 180°C, gas mark 4. Measure the flour into a bowl and rub in the fats until the mixture resembles fine breadcrumbs. Mix to a firm dough with the water, knead until smooth then roll out on a lightly floured surface. Cut out 24 circles with a fluted pastry cutter and use to line patty tins. Place a ½ teaspoonful of the marmalade in the bottom of each pastry case.

For the topping, measure all the ingredients into a mixing bowl and beat well until thoroughly blended. Spoon teaspoonfuls of the mixture on top of the marmalade so that the marmalade is sealed in the middle. Bake in the oven for about 35 minutes until the topping is a golden brown and the pastry is cooked underneath. Leave to cool in the tins for a few moments then lift out carefully with a knife and finish cooling on a cake rack.

Makes about 24

Yorkshire Cakes

These are delicious small tarts with a spongy filling.

Making time about 20 minutes
Cooking time about 20–25 minutes

8 oz/225 g (2 cups) plain (all-purpose) flour
2 oz/50 g (¹/₄ cup) lard
2 oz/50 g (¹/₄ cup) margarine
about 8 teaspoons water

Filling
raspberry jam

Topping
4 oz/100 g (¹/₂ cup) soft margarine
8 oz/225 g (1¹/₂ cups) caster (very fine granulated) sugar
2 eggs, beaten
4 oz/100 g (1 cup) semolina or ground rice
2 oz/50 g (¹/₃ cup) currants

Heat the oven to 400°F, 200°C, gas mark 6.

Measure the flour into a bowl and rub in the lard and margarine until the mixture resembles fine breadcrumbs. Mix to a firm dough with the water, knead until smooth then roll out on a lightly floured surface. Cut out 24 circles and use to line patty tins. Spoon half a teaspoonful of the jam into the bottom of each pastry case.

For the topping, measure all the ingredients into a mixing bowl and beat well until thoroughly blended then spoon teaspoonfuls of the mixture on top of the jam so that the jam is sealed in the middle. Bake in the oven for 20–25 minutes until the topping is golden brown and the pastry is cooked underneath. Allow to cool in the tins for a few moments then carefully lift out with a knife and finish cooling on a cake rack.

Makes about 24

Lemon Cream Strawberry Tarts

Fill these tarts just before serving as the cream filling soon begins to soften the pastry cases. The pastry cases can always be frozen ahead of time and then thawed and filled when required. *See photograph facing page 96.*

Making time about 20 minutes
Baking time about 15 minutes

> 4 oz/100 g (1 cup) plain (all-purpose) flour
> 1½ oz/40 g (3 tablespoons) butter
> 1½ oz/40 g (3 tablespoons) lard
> ½ oz/15 g (2 teaspoons) caster (very fine granulated) sugar
> 1 egg yolk

Filling
> ¼ pint/150 ml (⅔ cup) whipping (heavy) cream
> 3 good tablespoons lemon curd or lemon cheese, preferably home-made

Topping
> 18 small whole fresh strawberries

Heat the oven to 400°F, 200°C, gas mark 6.

Measure the flour into a bowl and rub in the fats until the mixture resembles fine breadcrumbs. Stir in the sugar and mix to a firm dough with the egg yolk. Roll out dough on a lightly floured surface, cut out 18 circles with a fluted pastry cutter and use to line two patty tins. Line each tart with a small piece of foil. Chill in the refrigerator for about 15 minutes then bake in the oven for about 15 minutes, until the pastry is cooked, removing the foil for the last 5 minutes to dry out the bottom of the pastry. Leave to cool in the tins for a few moments then carefully lift the pastry cases out on to a cake rack to finish cooling.

For the filling, whip the cream in a bowl until the mixture forms soft peaks then gently fold in the lemon curd. Spoon a generous teaspoonful of the cream into each of the pastry cases and top with a strawberry.

Makes 18

Banbury Cakes

The original recipe is still a closely guarded secret. This is a good attempt at copying that delicious filling for which Banbury cakes are famous.

Making time about 20 minutes
Baking time about 20 minutes

> *6 oz/175 g frozen puff pastry, thawed*

Filling
> *2 oz/50 g (¼ cup) butter*
> *1 oz/25 g (1 tablespoon) plain (all-purpose) flour*
> *2 oz/50 g (⅓ cup) demerara (brown) sugar*
> *2 tablespoons rum*
> *6 oz/175 g (¾ cup) mixed dried fruit*
> *1 teaspoon mixed spice (cinnamon, cloves, nutmeg, etc.)*
> *1 lightly beaten egg white and caster (very fine granulated) sugar to glaze*

Heat the oven to 450°F, 230°C, gas mark 8. Lightly grease two large baking sheets.

Roll out the pastry on a lightly floured surface to about ⅛-inch/3-mm thickness. Cut out rounds the size of a tea saucer, continuing until all the pastry has been used. This will make about 6 rounds.

For the filling, melt the butter in a pan, stir in the flour and cook for a minute then remove from the heat and stir in the sugar and rum. Beat well until smooth then stir in the remaining filling ingredients. Put a good tablespoon of the filling into the middle of each pastry round, wet the edges with water then fold in all the edges to the centre and seal together. Turn the cake over and roll it a little so that it forms an oval shape. Make three slits in the top of each cake with a sharp knife and lift on to the baking sheets.

Bake in the oven for about 15 minutes then remove and brush with egg white and sprinkle with a little caster sugar. Return to the oven for about a further 5 minutes until golden brown.

Makes 6

Chocolate Palmiers

Best eaten when freshly made. Good served with ice-cream.

Making time about 15 minutes
Baking time about 16 minutes

6 oz/175 g frozen puff pastry, thawed
2 oz/50 g (¹/₃ cup) demerara (brown) sugar
4 oz/100 g plain (semi-sweet) chocolate, melted

Heat the oven to 450°F, 230°C, gas mark 8. Lightly grease two large baking sheets.

Roll out the pastry on a lightly floured surface to a large oblong, and sprinkle evenly with half the sugar. Fold into three and roll out again and sprinkle with the remaining sugar and fold into three. Re-roll into an oblong 8 × 12 inches/ 20 × 30 cm. Fold the two short ends of the pastry into the middle, and the folds you have made into the middle again, then fold one half on to the other. Cut this sausage-shaped piece of pastry into about 16 slices, and arrange these flat on the prepared baking sheets so you can see the layers. Chill in the refrigerator for about 30 minutes.

Bake in the oven for 8 minutes, remove and turn the palmiers over then return to the oven for about a further 8 minutes so that they are golden brown on both sides. Lift off with a metal spatula and finish cooling on a cake rack. When cold dip each end in the melted chocolate and allow to set on a sheet of silicone paper.

Makes about 16 slices

Coffee and Chocolate Eclairs

These are quite one of my most favourite things to eat. The coffee filling makes them that extra bit more special. Be sure to thoroughly dry out the pastry cases during the baking before filling with cream, so that they are crisp to eat. Ideally they should be filled just before serving so that they retain this crispiness. *See photograph facing page 96.*

Making time about 30 minutes
Baking time about 25–30 minutes

> *2 oz/50 g (¼ cup) butter*
> *¼ pint/150 ml (⅔ cup) water*
> *2½ oz/65 g (½ cup generous) plain (all-purpose) flour*
> *2 eggs, beaten*

Filling
> *2 oz/50 g (⅓ cup generous) icing (powdered) sugar, sieved*
> *1 tablespoon coffee essence (extract)*
> *½ pint/300 ml (1⅓ cups) whipping (heavy) cream, whipped*

Topping
> *2 oz/50 g plain (semi-sweet) chocolate*
> *2 tablespoons water*
> *½ oz/15 g (1 tablespoon) butter*
> *3 oz/75 g (⅔ cup) icing (powdered) sugar, sieved*

Heat the oven to 425°F, 220°C, gas mark 7, and grease two large baking sheets.

For the pastry, measure the butter and water into a pan, slowly bring to the boil and allow the butter to melt. Remove from the heat and add the flour all at once and beat until it forms a soft ball. Gradually add the eggs, a little at a time, beating well to give a smooth shiny paste. Put the mixture into a piping bag fitted with a ½-inch/1.25-cm plain nozzle, and pipe 20 eclairs on to the baking sheets, leaving room for them to expand during cooking. Bake in the oven for 10 minutes then reduce the temperature to 375°F, 190°C, gas mark 5 and cook for a further 15–20 minutes until well risen and golden brown. Remove from the oven and split one side of each eclair with a knife to allow the steam to escape.

120

For the filling, fold the icing sugar and coffee essence into the cream. Pipe or spoon the cream into the middle of the eclairs. For the topping, put the chocolate, water and butter in a bowl and heat gently over a pan of simmering water until the mixture has melted. Remove from the heat and beat in the icing sugar until smooth. Pour chocolate sauce into a shallow dish and dip each eclair into the sauce to coat the top. Allow to set on a cake rack before serving.

Makes about 20 small eclairs

Baklava

Serve this pastry warm with whipped cream. Phyllo pastry is readily available from good Greek shops and delicatessens.

Making time about 10 minutes
Baking time about 30 minutes

8 oz/225 g phyllo pastry
4 oz/100 g (¹/₂ cup) unsalted butter, melted
grated rind and juice of 1 lemon
4 oz/100 g (1 cup) walnuts, finely chopped
1 oz/25 g (1 tablespoon) demerara (brown) sugar
whipped cream to serve

Syrup
¹/₄ pint/150 ml (²/₃ cup) water
8 oz/225 g (1¹/₃ cups) caster (very fine granulated) sugar

Heat the oven to 400°F, 200°C, gas mark 6. Lightly butter a 7 × 11-inch/ 17.5 × 27.5-cm Swiss roll tin.

Cut the pastry sheets in half so that they are roughly the size of the tin. Lay 1 sheet of pastry in the tin, brush with melted butter and continue until there are 8 layers of pastry in the tin. Brush the top layer with butter and sprinkle with lemon rind, nuts and sugar. Continue to add 8 more layers of pastry, brushing with melted butter between each layer. Brush the top with more melted butter, and cut with a very sharp knife into 16 equal sized pieces. Bake in the oven for about 30 minutes until pale golden brown. Remove from the oven and leave to cool in the tin.

For the syrup, measure the water and sugar into a pan, slowly bring to the boil and simmer for about 15 minutes without a lid to give a light syrup, remove from the heat, stir in the juice of the lemon, and pour over the baklava. Serve with whipped cream.

Serves 8

FOR THE BISCUIT TIN

Be sure to cool biscuits (cookies) thoroughly before putting them in a tin, other-wise they will be soggy, not lovely and crisp, by the next day. And you should never store cakes and biscuits together: again the biscuits would become soggy, taking moisture from the cakes. If there is little room in the biscuit tin, they can always be kept in a plastic container or bag and sealed.

Remember that if the lid has been accidentally left off the tin, biscuits or cookies can always be freshened up in a moderate oven for 10 minutes or so, and then cooled.

Oat and Almond Biscuits

These are rather soft-textured, and they are ideal to serve with coffee.

Making time about 10 minutes
Baking time about 15 minutes

4 oz/100 g (¹/₂ cup) soft margarine
3 oz/75 g (¹/₂ cup) light muscovado (brown) sugar
4 oz/100 g (1 cup) self-raising flour
4 oz/100 g (1³/₄ cups) porridge (rolled) oats
1 rounded tablespoon runny honey
1 egg, beaten

Topping
about 2 oz/50 g (¹/₂ cup) flaked (slivered) almonds

Heat the oven to 350°F, 180°C, gas mark 4. Lightly grease two large baking sheets.

Measure all the ingredients for the biscuits into a bowl and mix well until thoroughly blended. Spoon teaspoonfuls of the mixture on to the baking trays, leaving a little room for them to spread. Top each with a flaked almond then bake in the oven for about 15 minutes until golden brown.

Allow to cool on the trays for about 2 minutes, then lift off with a metal spatula and finish cooling on a cake rack.

Makes about 45

Almond Biscuits

These biscuits are really crunchy, and full of goodness.

Making time about 15 minutes
Baking time about 20 minutes

4 oz/100 g (½ cup) soft margarine
2 oz/50 g (⅓ cup) light muscovado (brown) sugar
2 oz/50 g (½ cup) blanched almonds, chopped
4 oz/100 g (1 cup) wholemeal (wholewheat) flour
1 tablespoon milk

Topping
   about 16 blanched almond halves

Heat the oven to 375°F, 190°C, gas mark 5. Lightly grease two large baking sheets.

Measure all the ingredients for the biscuits into a mixing bowl and work together until thoroughly mixed. Take teaspoonfuls of the mixture and roll into balls. Arrange on the prepared baking sheets, flatten slightly, and top with half an almond. Bake in the oven for about 20 minutes until golden brown.

Leave to cool on the trays for a few moments then lift off with a metal spatula and finish cooling on a cake rack.

Makes about 16

Special Muesli Biscuits

I find these are nicest made with home-made muesli (granola) as some of the bought mueslis tend to be rather sweet.

Making time about 10 minutes
Baking time about 15 minutes

4 oz/100 g (1/2 cup) butter
2 oz/50 g (1/3 cup) demerara (brown) sugar
1 good tablespoon golden syrup (light corn syrup)
4 oz/100 g (1 cup) self-raising flour
4 oz/100 g (2 cups) breakfast muesli (granola)
1 teaspoon bicarbonate of soda (baking soda)

Heat the oven to 325°F, 160°C, gas mark 3. Lightly grease two large baking sheets.

Put the butter, sugar and syrup in a pan and heat gently until the butter has melted. Measure the remaining ingredients into a large bowl then pour in the melted mixture and stir well until thoroughly mixed. Spoon teaspoonfuls of the mixture on the prepared baking sheet, leaving plenty of room for them to spread, and bake in the oven for about 15 minutes until golden brown.

Leave to cool for a few moments on the sheets then lift off with a metal spatula on to a cake rack to finish cooling.

Makes about 25

Treacle Black Jacks

These are simple to make and keep well in the cake tin, unless hungry children find them first of course!

Making time about 10 minutes
Baking time about 20–25 minutes

3 oz/75 g (6 tablespoons) soft margarine
3 oz/75 g (³/4 cup) light muscovado (brown) sugar
1¹/2 oz/40 g (1¹/2 tablespoons) black treacle (molasses)
6 oz/175 g (2¹/3 cups) porridge (rolled) oats
¹/2 level teaspoon ground ginger

Heat the oven to 375°F, 190°C, gas mark 5. Grease a 7-inch/17.5-cm round sandwich tin and line with a piece of greased greaseproof paper.

Melt the margarine in a pan with the sugar and treacle. Remove from the heat and stir in the oats and ginger. Mix thoroughly then press into the prepared tin. Bake in the oven for 20–25 minutes until beginning to get firm to the touch.

Remove from the oven and mark into 8 wedges. Leave to cool in the tin, then turn out and discard paper.

Makes 8 wedges

Special Flapjacks

A very dear lady in the village gave me this recipe. I tried it at home and it went down a treat with the family.

Making time 10 minutes
Baking time about 30 minutes

   4 oz/100 g (1/2 cup) butter
   4 oz/100 g (4 tablespoons) golden syrup (light corn syrup)
   2 oz/50 g (1/3 cup) demerara (brown) sugar
   4 oz/100 g (3/4 cup) porridge (rolled) oats
   2 oz/50 g (1/2 cup) flaked (slivered) almonds

Heat the oven to 350°F, 180°C, gas mark 4. Line a 7 × 11-inch/ 17.5 × 27.5-cm Swiss roll tin with silicone paper.

Measure the butter, syrup and sugar into a small pan and heat gently until the butter has melted. Measure the oats and flaked almonds into a mixing bowl and pour the melted mixture over them. Stir well until thoroughly mixed then spread out evenly on the bottom of the prepared tin. Bake in the oven for about 30 minutes until golden brown.

Remove from the oven and mark into 16 squares. Leave in the tin to become cold before lifting out with a metal spatula. Store in an airtight tin.

Makes about 16 squares

Banana Flapjacks

Any over-ripe bananas which may be sitting in your fruit bowl can be used for this recipe.

Making time about 10 minutes
Baking time about 35–40 minutes

3 oz/75 g (6 tablespoons) hard margarine
2 tablespoons honey
4 oz/100 g (1 cup) light muscovado (brown) sugar
1 large banana, mashed
6 oz/175 g (2¹/₃ cups) porridge (rolled) oats

Heat the oven to 350°F, 180°C, gas mark 4. Grease a 7 × 11-inch/ 17.5 × 27.5-cm Swiss roll tin.

Measure the margarine, honey and sugar into a pan and heat gently until the margarine has melted and the sugar dissolved. Remove from the heat and stir in the banana and oats and mix thoroughly. Press into the prepared tin and level out evenly. Bake in the oven for about 35–40 minutes until pale golden brown.

Leave to cool for a few minutes then mark into 16 fingers and allow to finish cooling in the tin before lifting out.

Makes 16 fingers

Florentines

I usually have to make double the quantity of these very special biscuits – they disappear so quickly. *See photograph facing page 97.*

Making time about 25 minutes
Baking time 8–10 minutes

  2 oz/50 g (¹/₄ cup) butter
  2 oz/50 g (¹/₃ cup) demerara (brown) sugar
  2 oz/50 g (2 tablespoons) golden syrup (light corn syrup)
  2 oz/50 g (¹/₂ cup) plain (all-purpose) flour
  4 glacé (candied) cherries, finely chopped
  2 oz/50 g (¹/₂ cup) currants
  2 oz/50 g (¹/₂ cup) chopped nuts such as almonds and walnuts

Topping
  6 oz/175 g plain (semi-sweet) chocolate, melted

Heat the oven to 350°F, 180°C, gas mark 4. Grease two or three large baking sheets.

Measure the butter, sugar and golden syrup into a small pan and heat gently until the butter has melted. Measure the flour, cherries, currants and nuts into a mixing bowl, pour over melted mixture and stir well until thoroughly mixed. Spoon teaspoonfuls of the mixture on to the prepared baking sheets, leaving plenty of space for them to spread, and bake in the oven for 8–10 minutes until golden brown.

Allow to cool for a few moments then carefully lift off the trays with a metal spatula on to a cake rack. Watch that the florentines don't become too cool, when they will be difficult to lift off the baking tray. If this does happen, put them back in the oven for a minute so they warm through and will then lift off more easily. It may not be possible to bake them all at the same time so do a few at a time until all the mixture has been used.

When cold, spread a little melted chocolate over the flat base of each florentine, mark a zigzag in the chocolate with a fork and leave to set, chocolate side up, on the cooling rack. Store in an airtight tin.

Makes about 20

Cinnamon Fairings

Really crunchy biscuits, the amount made will vary with the size of cutter used.

Making time about 15 minutes
Baking time about 15 minutes

4 oz/100 g (1 cup) semolina
5 oz/150 g (1¼ cups) self-raising flour
4 oz/100 g (⅔ cup) caster (very fine granulated) sugar
½ level teaspoon ground cinnamon
4 oz/100 g (½ cup) soft margarine
1 egg, beaten
a little caster (very fine granulated) sugar, to sprinkle on top

Heat the oven to 350°F, 180°C, gas mark 4. Lightly grease two large baking sheets.

Measure all the dry ingredients into a bowl and rub in margarine until the mixture resembles fine breadcrumbs. Bind together with the egg to give a soft dough. Turn out on to a lightly floured surface and knead until smooth. Roll out to a good ⅓-inch/3-mm thickness and cut out with biscuit cutters. Lift on to the prepared baking sheets with a spatula, re-roll pastry trimmings and cut out until all pastry has been used. Bake in the oven for about 15 minutes until just beginning to brown at the edges.

Leave to cool on the sheets for a moment then lift off with a palette knife and finish cooling on a cake rack. Sprinkle with a little caster sugar before serving.

Makes about 50

Cinnamon Crispy Biscuits

Lovely crunchy biscuits, always popular in our biscuit tin.

Making time 15 minutes
Baking time about 12 minutes

8 oz/225 g (1 cup) soft margarine
8 oz/225 g (1¹/₄ cups) demerara (brown) sugar
8 oz/225 g (2 cups) self-raising flour
¹/₂ level teaspoon ground mixed spice (cinnamon, cloves, nutmeg, etc.)
2 level teaspoons ground cinnamon
1 egg, beaten

Heat the oven to 400°F, 200°C, gas mark 6. Lightly grease two to three large baking sheets.

Measure all the ingredients into a large mixing bowl and work together until thoroughly mixed. Spoon teaspoonfuls of the mixture on to the baking sheets, leaving room for them to spread, and bake in the oven for about 12 minutes until golden brown.

Leave to cool on the sheets for a moment then lift off with a spatula and finish cooling on a cake rack.

Makes about 38

Lemon Biscuits

As a variation add orange instead of lemon or, for spiced biscuits, add ½ teaspoon ground mixed spice (cinnamon, cloves, nutmeg, etc.)

Making and chilling time 40 minutes
Baking time 15 minutes

4 oz/100 g (½ cup) soft margarine
3 oz/75 g (½ cup) caster (very fine granulated) sugar
6 oz/175 g (1½ cups) plain (all-purpose) flour
finely grated rind of 1 lemon
a little milk to glaze
caster (very fine granulated) sugar to sprinkle on top

Heat the oven to 375°F, 190°C, gas mark 5. Lightly grease a large baking sheet.

Cream the margarine and sugar until light then work in the flour and lemon rind to give a soft dough. Wrap in clingfilm and chill in the refrigerator for about 30 minutes.

Roll out to an oblong, 5 × 15 inches/12.5 × 37.5 cm, on a lightly floured surface. Brush with milk and sprinkle with caster sugar. Divide into 30 fingers then lift on to the prepared sheet with a metal spatula. Bake in the oven for about 15 minutes until tinged with golden brown at the edges. Lift on to a cake rack to cool.

Makes about 30

Lemon Star Biscuits

My children adore these. If liked, ice (glaze) them with a little lemon icing made with the juice of the lemon and icing sugar.

Making time about 15 minutes
Baking time about 10 minutes

4 oz/100 g (¹/₂ cup) soft margarine
4 oz/100 g (²/₃ cup) caster (very fine granulated) sugar
7 oz/200 g (1³/₄ cups) plain (all-purpose) flour
1 oz/25 g (¹/₄ cup) semolina
grated rind of 1 lemon
1 egg, beaten
caster (very fine granulated) sugar to sprinkle on top

Heat the oven to 375°F, 190°C, gas mark 5. Lightly grease two to three large baking sheets.

Measure all the ingredients into a large mixing bowl and work together until thoroughly blended. Turn out on to a lightly floured surface and knead until smooth. Roll out to ¹/₈-inch/3-mm thickness, then cut out with a star-shaped cutter (or any other 2-inch/5-cm cutter you have). Lift on to the baking sheets with a metal spatula, re-roll and cut out the trimmings until all the dough has been used.

Bake in the oven for about 10 minutes until just beginning to tinge with golden brown. Sprinkle with caster sugar and lift on to a cake rack with a palette knife to cool.

Makes about 36, depending on the cutter you use

Lemon Shortbread

This really is quite one of my favourite shortbreads. It keeps extremely well in an airtight tin and is delicious to serve with a cup of coffee. *See photograph facing page 144.*

Making time about 10 minutes
Baking time about 35 minutes

> 4 oz/100 g (¹/₂ cup) butter, softened
> 2 oz/50 g (¹/₃ cup) caster (very fine granulated) sugar
> 4 oz/100 g (1 cup) plain (all-purpose) flour
> 2 oz/50 g (¹/₂ cup scant) cornflour (cornstarch)
> grated rind of 1 large lemon
> caster (very fine granulated) sugar to sprinkle on top

Heat the oven to 325°F, 160°C, gas mark 3, and lightly grease a 7-inch/17.5-cm square tin.

Cream the butter and sugar together in a mixing bowl until light and then work in the flours and lemon rind. Knead well until smooth. Press the mixture into the prepared tin, level the top, then bake in the oven for about 35 minutes or until a pale golden brown.

Remove from the oven and mark into 12 fingers then leave in the tin to become quite cold before lifting out with a metal spatula on to a cake rack. Sprinkle with caster sugar before serving.

Makes 12 fingers

Chocolate Shortbread Fingers

These are always the first to disappear out of the tin! *See photograph facing page 97.*

Making time about 20 minutes
Baking time about 20 minutes

   8 oz/225 g (1 cup) soft margarine
   2 oz/50 g (⅓ cup) icing (powdered) sugar
   8 oz/225 g (2 cups) plain (all-purpose) flour

Chocolate Topping
   4 oz/100 g plain (semi-sweet) chocolate, melted

Heat the oven to 325°F, 160°C, gas mark 3. Lightly grease two large baking sheets.

Measure all the ingredients for the shortbread into a mixing bowl and rub in the margarine until the mixture resembles fine breadcrumbs. Work the mixture together to form a soft dough, then knead well until smooth. Put the mixture in a piping bag fitted with a large star-shaped nozzle and pipe out into 2–3-inch/5–7.5-cm lengths on the prepared baking sheets. Bake in the oven for about 20 minutes until just tinged with golden brown then remove from the oven. Leave to cool for a few moments on the sheets then lift off with a metal spatula and finish cooling on a cake rack.

When quite cold dip the fingers into the melted chocolate so that just the ends are coated and leave to set on a cake rack.

Makes about 30 fingers

Chocolate Biscuits

Lovely, light crunchy biscuits that keep well in an airtight tin.

Making time about 15 minutes
Baking time about 10 minutes

> *4 oz/100 g (¹/₂ cup) soft margarine*
> *2 oz/50 g (¹/₃ cup) caster (very fine granulated) sugar*
> *4 oz/100 g (1 cup) self-raising flour*
> *1 oz/25 g (¹/₃ cup) cocoa*

Heat the oven to 375°F, 190°C, gas mark 5. Lightly grease two large baking sheets.

Measure the margarine and sugar into a bowl and cream together until light. Work in the flour and cocoa until all has been added. (This is done most easily by kneading the mixture together with your hands until smooth.) Take teaspoonfuls of the mixture and roll into small balls. Arrange on the prepared baking sheets, flatten down with a fork which has been dipped in cold water and bake in the oven for about 10 minutes.

Leave to cool on the baking sheets for a few moments then lift off and on to a cake rack with a metal spatula to finish cooling.

Makes 36

Burnt Butter Biscuits

These have a divine flavour, and thus you must use butter – margarine will not do. They don't look too exciting but are quite one of our favourites. *See photograph facing page 144.*

Making time 10 minutes
Baking time about 15 minutes

4 oz/100 g (¹⁄₂ cup) butter
4 oz/100 g (²⁄₃ cup) caster (very fine granulated) sugar
1 egg, beaten
2 drops vanilla essence (extract)
5 oz/150 g (1¹⁄₄ cups) self-raising flour

Topping
12 walnut halves, cut in half

Heat the oven to 350°F, 180°C, gas mark 4. Lightly grease two to three large baking sheets.

Put the butter in a pan, melt and allow to boil gently for about 3 minutes until it becomes golden brown. Allow to cool.

Measure all the remaining ingredients into a bowl then beat in the cool butter until thoroughly blended. Spoon teaspoonfuls of the mixture on to the prepared sheets, leaving room for them to spread. Bake in the oven for 8 minutes, then top with a piece of walnut and return to the oven for about a further 7 minutes until a dark golden brown. Lift on to a cake rack with a metal spatula to cool.

Makes 24

Traditional Dutch Butter Biscuits

These biscuits really should be made with butter as the flavour of margarine doesn't do them justice.

Making time about 15 minutes
Baking time about 10 minutes

8 oz/225 g (1 cup) unsalted butter, softened
4 oz/100 g (²/₃ cup) caster (very fine granulated) sugar
1 egg yolk
4 oz/100 g (1 cup) plain (all-purpose) flour
4 oz/100 g (1 cup) self-raising flour
3 oz/75 g (³/₄ cup) ground almonds
a little icing (powdered) sugar to dust

Heat the oven to 375°F, 190°C, gas mark 5. Lightly grease two to three large baking sheets. Measure all the ingredients, except the icing sugar, into a large mixing bowl and work together until thoroughly mixed and smooth (this can be done most quickly in a processor or food mixer). Place the mixture in a piping bag fitted with a large rose nozzle and pipe the mixture into rounds on the prepared trays. Bake in the oven for about 10 minutes until just beginning to colour at the edges.

Leave to cool on the trays for a few moments then lift off with a metal spatula and finish cooling on a cake rack. Serve dusted with a little icing sugar.

Makes about 20

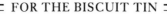

Danish Lace Biscuits

Very thin almondy biscuits, which are good to serve with cold desserts.

Making time 15 minutes
Baking time about 12 minutes

   2 oz/50 g (¹/₂ cup) blanched almonds, chopped
   3 oz/75 g (³/₄ cup) plain (all-purpose) flour
   3 oz/75 g (¹/₂ cup) caster (very fine granulated) sugar
   3 oz/75 g (6 tablespoons) soft margarine

Heat the oven to 350°F, 180°C, gas mark 4. Lightly grease two large baking sheets.

Measure all the ingredients into a bowl and work together with a wooden spoon to form a firm dough. Knead gently until smooth. Take teaspoonfuls of the mixture, roll into balls and arrange on the baking sheets, leaving room for them to spread. Press down with a fork to flatten them and reshape to a round with the back of the fork. Bake in the oven for about 12 minutes until just beginning to turn golden brown at the edges.

Leave to cool on the sheets for a moment then lift on to a cake rack with a metal spatula to finish cooling.

Makes about 25

Abbey Biscuits

Delicious, always a favourite with a cup of coffee. *See photograph facing page 97.*

Making time 15 minutes
Baking time about 20 minutes

5 oz/150 g (1¼ cups) plain (all-purpose) flour
5 oz/150 g (10 tablespoons) soft margarine
5 oz/150 g (¾ cup) caster (very fine granulated) sugar
4 oz/100 g (1¾ cups) porridge (rolled) oats
1 tablespoon milk
1 rounded tablespoon golden syrup (light corn syrup)
1 teaspoon bicarbonate of soda (baking soda)

Heat the oven to 325°F, 160°C, gas mark 3. Lightly grease two large baking sheets.

Measure all the ingredients into a bowl and work together until thoroughly blended. Take teaspoonfuls of the mixture, roll into balls, and arrange on the prepared baking trays leaving room for them to spread. Bake in the oven for about 20 minutes until golden brown.

Leave to cool on the trays for a few moments then lift on to a cake rack with a metal spatula to cool.

Makes about 40

Hurdon Farmhouse Biscuits

These biscuits are a bit fiddly to prepare as the porridge oats don't stick easily – but it's worth pesevering as the end result looks good and tastes delicious. *See photograph facing page 144.*

Making time about 25 minutes
Baking time about 15 minutes

> *12 oz/350 g (3 cups) self-raising flour*
> *8 oz/225 g (1 cup) soft margarine*
> *6 oz/175 g (1 cup) caster (very fine granulated) sugar*
> *1 large egg, beaten*
> *1 oz/25 g (½ cup scant) porridge (rolled) oats, to coat*

Heat the oven to 350°F, 180°C, gas mark 4. Lightly grease two or three large baking sheets.

Measure the flour into a large mixing bowl and rub in the margarine until the mixture resembles fine breadcrumbs. Stir in the sugar and bind to a dough with the beaten egg. Knead until smooth. Take teaspoonfuls of the mixture and roll them into balls. Press the balls down into the porridge oats to flatten them into a rounds and coat lightly with the oats. Arrange on the prepared baking sheets and bake in the oven for about 15 minutes until pale golden brown.

Allow to cool on the sheets for a few moments then lift off with a metal spatula and finish cooling on a cake rack.

Makes about 50

Cherry and Coconut Biscuits

Very pretty biscuits, and you must take care not to over-bake them.

Making time 20 minutes
Baking time about 15 minutes

> 4 oz/100 g (½ cup) soft margarine
> 4 oz/100 g (⅔ cup) caster (very fine granulated) sugar
> 1 egg, beaten
> 8 oz/225 g (2 cups) self-raising flour
> a little milk
> about 3 oz/75 g (1 cup) desiccated (shredded) coconut
> 8 glacé (candied) cherries, quartered

Heat the oven to 350°F, 180°C, gas mark 4. Lightly grease two large baking sheets.

Measure the margarine, sugar, egg and flour into a bowl and work together to form a soft dough. Turn out on to a lightly floured surface and knead until smooth then roll out to ⅛-inch/3-mm thickness and cut into rounds with a 2-inch/5-cm fluted cutter. Brush with milk, sprinkle with coconut and top with a piece of cherry. Re-roll the trimmings until all the dough has been used. Arrange on the baking sheets and bake in the oven for about 15 minutes until just beginning to tinge with colour.

Lift on to a cake rack with a metal spatula to cool.

Makes 32

Ginger Thins

A special ginger biscuit that is good to serve with ice-creams and sorbets (sherbets).

Making time 15 minutes
Baking time about 20 minutes

4 oz/100 g (4 tablespoons) golden syrup (light corn syrup)
2 oz/50 g (¼ cup) hard margarine
1 oz/25 g (1 tablespoon) demerara (brown) sugar
4 oz/100 g (1 cup) plain (all-purpose) flour
1½ level teaspoons ground ginger
½ level teaspoon bicarbonate of soda (baking soda)
½ level teaspoon ground mixed spice (cinnamon, cloves, nutmeg, etc.)

Heat the oven to 350°F, 180°C, gas mark 4. Lightly grease two large baking sheets.

Heat the syrup, margarine and sugar in a pan until margarine has melted. Measure remaining ingredients into a bowl, add melted mixture and beat well until thoroughly blended. Spoon teaspoonfuls of the mixture on to the baking sheets, leaving room for them to spread. Bake in the oven for about 20 minutes until dark golden brown.

Lift on to a cake rack with a metal spatula to cool.

Makes about 28

Right: Hurdon Farmhouse Biscuits (page 142), Lemon Shortbread (page 135) and Burnt Butter Biscuits (page 138).

Ginger Cookies

These can easily be fitted in with the rest of your plans for the day. The mixture can be prepared and then allowed to chill whilst you are out shopping and then be baked when you get back.

Making time about 10 minutes
Baking time about 10 minutes

8 oz/225 g (2 cups) self-raising flour
2 level teaspoons ground ginger
6 oz/175 g (³/₄ cup) soft margarine
6 oz/175 g (1¹/₂ cups) light muscovado (brown) sugar

Heat the oven to 375°F, 190°C, gas mark 5. Lightly grease two large baking sheets.

Measure the flour and ginger into a bowl and rub in the margarine until the mixture resembles fine breadcrumbs. Stir in the sugar then bind together to form a firm dough. Knead until smooth then roll into a sausage shape about 2 inches/5 cm in diameter. Wrap in clingfilm and chill in the refrigerator until really firm.

Slice the roll into about 24 thin slices and arrange, well spaced, on the prepared baking sheets. Bake in the oven for about 10 minutes until pale golden brown at the edges. Remove from the oven and leave to cool on the sheets for a few moments then lift off with a metal spatula and finish cooling on a cake rack.

Makes about 24 cookies

Left: Welsh Currant Loaf (page 161) and All-in-One Brioches (page 166).

Crunchy Sultana Gingernuts

Muscovado sugar is an unrefined sugar and adds a lovely flavour when used in baking.

Making time about 15 minutes
Baking time about 20 minutes

  12 oz/350 g (3 cups) self-raising flour
  4 oz/100 g (1 cup) light muscovado (brown) sugar
  4 oz/100 g (⅔ cup) demerara (brown) sugar
  1 teaspoon bicarbonate of soda (baking soda)
  3 good teaspoons ground ginger
  1 egg, beaten
  4 oz/100 g (½ cup) hard margarine
  1 good tablespoon golden syrup (light corn syrup)
  2 oz/50 g (½ cup scant) sultanas (golden raisins)

Heat the oven to 325°F, 160°C, gas mark 3. Lightly grease two large baking sheets.

Mix all the dry ingredients together in a bowl and add the beaten egg. Heat the margarine and syrup in a pan until just melted then pour into the flour mixture with the sultanas and mix well until thoroughly blended. Take teaspoonfuls of the mixture and roll into balls. Arrange the balls on the prepared baking sheets, leaving room for them to spread, then bake in the oven for about 20 minutes until golden brown.

Leave to cool on the sheets for a few moments then lift off and on to a cake rack with a metal spatula to finish cooling.

Makes about 50

146

Walnut Spice Shorties

Delicious crisp spiced fingers. Store in an airtight tin.

Making time about 10 minutes
Baking time about 25 minutes

6 oz/175 g (³/4 cup) soft margarine
8 oz/225 g (2 cups) light muscovado (brown) sugar
8 oz/225 g (2 cups) self-raising flour
1 level teaspoon mixed spice (cinnamon, cloves, nutmeg, etc.)
2 oz/50 g (¹/2 cup) chopped walnuts

Heat the oven to 350°F, 180°C, gas mark 4. Lightly grease a 7 × 11-inch/ 17.5 × 27.5-cm Swiss roll tin.

Cream together the margarine and sugar in a large mixing bowl until light and fluffy. Gradually work in the flour, spice and walnuts (I find it best to do this with my hands). Turn into the prepared tin, spread out evenly. Bake in the oven for about 25 minutes, then remove.

Mark into 16 fingers and allow to cool in the tin. When cold lift out of tin and store in an airtight container.

Makes 16 fingers

Peanut Butter Cookies

These crunchy cookies are a great favourite with the children.

Making time 10 minutes
Baking time about 20 minutes

> 4 oz/100 g (1 cup) self-raising flour
> 2 oz/50 g (⅓ cup) caster (very fine granulated) sugar
> 2 oz/50 g (½ cup) light muscovado (brown) sugar
> 2 oz/50 g (¼ cup) soft margarine
> 3 level tablespoons crunchy peanut butter
> 1 egg, beaten

Heat the oven to 350°F, 180°C, gas mark 4. Lightly grease two large baking sheets.

Measure all the ingredients into a bowl and work together until thoroughly blended. Take teaspoonfuls of the mixture, roll into balls and arrange on the prepared baking sheets, leaving room for them to spread. Bake in the oven for about 20 minutes until golden brown.

Lift on to a cake rack with a metal spatula to cool.

Makes about 35

Treacle Cookies

These have a strong treacley flavour, and are very quick and easy.

Making time 15 minutes
Baking time 12 minutes

 1½ oz/40 g (3 tablespoons) hard margarine
 1½ oz/40 g (⅓ cup) dark soft brown sugar
 1 rounded tablespoon golden syrup (light corn syrup)
 1 rounded tablespoon black treacle (molasses)
 4 oz/100 g (1 cup) plain (all-purpose) flour
 1 level teaspoon ground mixed spice (cinnamon, cloves, nutmeg, etc.)
 ½ level teaspoon bicarbonate of soda (baking soda)
 4 tablespoons milk
 juice of ½ lemon

Heat the oven to 375°F, 190°C, gas mark 5. Lightly grease a large baking sheet.

Put the margarine, sugar, syrup and treacle into a small pan and heat gently until margarine has melted and sugar has dissolved. Measure the remaining ingredients into a bowl then add the melted mixture, and mix well until thoroughly blended. Spoon teaspoonfuls of the mixture on to the prepared baking sheet, leaving a little room for them to spread. Bake in the oven for about 12 minutes.

Allow to cool on the sheet for a moment then lift on to a cake rack with a metal spatula to finish cooling.

Makes about 26 cookies

Cheese Straws

Always popular with those who do not have a particularly sweet tooth, these are good to serve at a drinks party.

Making time about 10 minutes
Baking time about 10 minutes

4 oz/100 g (1 cup) self-raising flour
4 oz/100 g (1 cup) wholemeal (wholewheat) flour
salt
freshly ground black pepper
4 oz/100 g (½ cup) margarine
4 oz/100 g (1 cup) well flavoured Cheddar cheese, grated
a little beaten egg

Heat the oven to 400°F, 200°C, gas mark 6. Lightly grease two to three baking sheets.

Measure the flours, salt and pepper into a bowl and rub in the margarine until the mixture resembles fine breadcrumbs. Stir in the cheese, then add sufficient egg to give a firm dough. Turn out on to a lightly floured surface and knead until smooth.

Roll out to ¼-inch/6-mm thickness and cut into narrow strips. Arrange on the baking sheets and bake in the oven for about 10 minutes until just beginning to tinge with colour.

Leave to cool on the trays for a few moments then lift off with a metal spatula and finish cooling on a cake rack.

Cheesey Biscuits

Cheese is always very popular served after a meal, particular with the male members of the family. I like to have a few of these biscuits stored away in an airtight tin to serve with a selection of cheese.

Making time about 10 minutes
Baking time about 20 minutes

4 oz/100 g (¹/₂ cup) soft margarine
2 oz/50 g (¹/₂ cup) semolina
2 oz/50 g (¹/₂ cup) self-raising flour
2 oz/50 g (¹/₂ cup) wholemeal (wholewheat) flour
3 oz/75 g (³/₄ cup) well flavoured Cheddar cheese, grated
salt
¹/₂ teaspoon mustard powder
generous pinch of cayenne pepper

Heat the oven to 350°F, 180°C, gas mark 4. Lightly grease two baking sheets.

Measure all the ingredients into a mixing bowl and work together until thoroughly blended and smooth. Knead well then roll into a sausage shape about 6 inches/15 cm long. Wrap in clingfilm and chill in the refrigerator until firm.

Cut the roll into about 20 slices and arrange on the baking sheets. Bake in the oven for about 20 minutes until golden brown. Leave to cool on the sheets for a few moments then lift off with a metal spatula and finish cooling on a cake rack.

Makes about 20

BREADS,
TEABREADS
AND SCONES

Scones are so quick and inexpensive to make, and I find them the most useful recipe of this section. They can be made and baked in 20 minutes, which is a nice thought when unexpected guests arrive for tea. If liked, you can leave out the fruit, and serve with strawberry or cherry jam and cream.

Home-made breads add variety to tea, and are nice sliced and toasted later in the week. The home-made granary rolls are full of goodness, and taste very much better than bought.

Gingerbread

This recipe gives a moist, well flavoured gingerbread. It is rather an old-fashioned recipe using lard, but is very good. I always store this gingerbread for at least 3 days before I cut it, as it improves with keeping.

Making time about 5 minutes
Baking time about 45 minutes

8 oz/225 g (2 cups) self-raising flour
1 teaspoon mixed spice (cinnamon, cloves, nutmeg, etc.)
1 teaspoon ground ginger
5 oz/150 g (5 tablespoons) golden syrup (light corn syrup)
5 oz/150 g (5 tablespoons) black treacle (molasses)
4 oz/100 g (1 cup) dark muscovado (brown) sugar
4 oz/100 g (1/2 cup) lard
2 eggs, beaten
2 tablespoons milk

Heat the oven to 325°F, 160°C, gas mark 3. Grease and line with greased greaseproof paper an 8-inch/20-cm square tin.

Measure the flour, mixed spice and ginger into a large mixing bowl. Heat the syrup, treacle, sugar and lard over a low heat until the lard has just melted then add to the dry ingredients with the eggs and milk. Beat well until thoroughly blended then pour into the prepared tin, level out evenly and bake in the oven for about 45 minutes until the gingerbread is beginning to shrink back slightly from the sides of the tin.

Remove from the oven and leave to cool completely in the tin. Remove and discard the paper then store in an airtight tin for about 3 days until required.

Dark Gooey Gingerbread

This is a lovely moist gingerbread which improves with keeping. *Do* expect it to sink in the middle!

Making time 15 minutes
Baking time 1½–2 hours

4 oz/100 g (½ cup) margarine
4 oz/100 g (1 cup) dark muscovado (brown) sugar
6 oz/175 g (6 tablespoons) black treacle (molasses)
6 oz/175 g (6 tablespoons) golden syrup (light corn syrup)
8 oz/225 g (2 cups) plain (all-purpose) flour
½ level teaspoon bicarbonate of soda (baking soda)
2 level teaspoons ground cinnamon
3 level teaspoons ground ginger
1½ level teaspoons ground mixed spice (cinnamon, cloves, nutmeg, etc.)
3 eggs, beaten

Heat the oven to 325°F, 160°C, gas mark 3. Grease and line a 2-lb/900-g loaf tin with greased greaseproof paper.

Measure the margarine, sugar, treacle and syrup into a pan, and heat gently until margarine has melted and sugar has dissolved. Put the dry ingredients into a large mixing bowl, add the melted mixture and the eggs and beat well until thoroughly blended. Pour the mixture into the prepared tin and bake in the oven for 1½–2 hours. Test with a warm fine skewer: if the skewer comes out clean, then the cake is done.

Allow to cool in the tin. Remove the paper and keep in an airtight tin for a few days before serving, which gives it chance to mature.

Mild Ginger Loaf

This is very easy to make by the melting method. I often have stem ginger left on the larder shelf after Christmas, and this is one of my favourite ways of using it up. Best to eat within 2 days of baking.

Making time about 20 minutes
Baking time about 45 minutes

4 oz/100 g (1/2 cup) hard margarine
4 oz/100 g (1 cup) light muscovado (brown) sugar
2 level tablespoons black treacle (molasses)
8 oz/225 g (2 cups) self-raising flour
1 level teaspoon baking powder
1 level teaspoon ground ginger
2 oz/50 g stem (preserved) ginger, well drained and chopped
2 eggs, beaten

Heat the oven to 325°F, 160°C, gas mark 3. Grease and line a 1-lb/450-g loaf tin with greased greaseproof paper.

Measure the margarine, sugar and treacle into a pan and heat gently until the margarine has melted. Put all the dry ingredients in a mixing bowl, add melted mixture, chopped ginger and eggs and beat well for a minute until thoroughly blended. Pour into the prepared tin and bake in the oven for about 45 minutes until well risen. Test with a warm fine skewer: if the skewer comes out clean, then the cake is done.

Allow to cool in the tin for about 5 minutes, then turn out, remove paper and finish cooling on a cake rack. Serve cut in slices, with butter.

Orange and Walnut Loaf

Serve this loaf in slices, alone or spread with butter. For a change add currants instead of the candied peel, and lemon rind and juice instead of the orange. Both combinations are delicious.

Making time about 10 minutes
Baking time about 1 hour

6 oz/175 g (1½ cups) self-raising flour
1 level teaspoon baking powder
grated rind and juice of 1 large orange
2 oz/50 g (½ cup) walnuts, chopped
2 oz/50 g (⅓ cup) candied peel, chopped
3 oz/75 g (6 tablespoons) soft margarine
3 oz/75 g (¾ cup) light muscovado (brown) sugar
1 egg, beaten
3 tablespoons milk

Heat the oven to 350°F, 180°C, gas mark 4. Grease and line a 1-lb/450-g loaf tin with greaseproof paper.

Measure all the ingredients into a large bowl and beat well until thoroughly blended. Turn into the prepared tin and bake for about 1 hour until well risen. Test with a warm skewer: if the skewer comes out clean the loaf is done.

Leave to cool in the tin for about 15 minutes, then turn out, remove the paper and finish cooling on a cake rack.

Chocolate and Orange Loaf

This is beautifully moist and can be eaten happily without any butter.

Making time about 20 minutes
Baking time about 1 hour

6 oz/175 g (¾ cup) soft margarine
6 oz/175 g (1 cup) caster (very fine granulated) sugar
6 oz/175 g (1½ cups) self-raising flour
1 level teaspoon baking powder
grated rind of 1 orange
3 eggs, beaten
2 tablespoons milk

Chocolate Topping
2 oz/50 g (¼ cup) hard margarine
2 tablespoons cocoa, sieved
1 tablespoon golden syrup (light corn syrup)

Heat the oven to 375°F, 190°C, gas mark 5. Grease and line a 2-lb/900-g loaf tin with greased greaseproof paper.

Put all the ingredients for the loaf in a large mixing bowl and beat well until thoroughly blended. Turn the mixture into the prepared tin and bake in the oven for about 1 hour until well risen and the top springs back when lightly pressed with a finger. Leave to cool in the tin then turn out and remove the paper.

For the chocolate topping, heat the margarine, cocoa and syrup in a pan, stirring until well mixed, then remove from the heat. Allow to cool until just beginning to set, then spread evenly over the top of the loaf. Serve in slices.

Banana Loaf

A delicious cut-and-come-again loaf that really tastes of banana.

Making time about 10 minutes
Baking time about 1½ hours

2 ripe bananas, mashed down with a fork
4 oz/100 g (1 cup) wholemeal (wholewheat) flour
5 oz/150 g (1¼ cups) self-raising flour
2 level teaspoons baking powder
4 oz/100 g (½ cup) soft margarine
6 oz/175 g (1½ cups) light muscovado (brown) sugar
2 large eggs, beaten
5-oz/142-g carton (⅔ cup) natural yoghurt
5 oz/150 g (1 cup) currants
2 tablespoons milk

Heat the oven to 350°F, 180°C, gas mark 4. Grease and line a 2-lb/900-g loaf tin with greased greaseproof paper.

Measure all the ingredients into a large mixing bowl and beat well until thoroughly blended. Turn into the prepared tin and bake in the oven for about 1½ hours until well risen. Test with a warm fine skewer: if the skewer comes out clean, then the cake is done.

Leave to cool in the tin for about 15 minutes then turn out, remove the paper, and finish cooling on a cake rack. Serve in slices, with butter.

Glacé Fruit Loaf

Be sure to wash and dry the glacé (candied) fruits thoroughly otherwise they do have a tendency to sink!

Making time about 5 minutes
Baking time about 40–50 minutes

> 4 oz/100 g (½ cup) glacé (candied) fruits, chopped, rinsed and thoroughly dried
> 4 oz/100 g (1 cup) self-raising flour
> 3 oz/75 g (6 tablespoons) soft margarine
> 3 oz/75 g (½ cup) caster (very fine granulated) sugar
> 2 eggs, beaten
> finely grated rind of 1 small orange
> 1 oz/25 g (¼ cup) ground rice

Heat the oven to 350°F, 180°C, gas mark 4. Grease and line with greased greaseproof paper a 1-lb/450-g loaf tin.

Measure all the ingredients into a large bowl and beat well until thoroughly blended. Turn into the prepared tin, level out evenly and bake in the oven for about 40–50 minutes until well risen. Test with a warm fine skewer: if the skewer comes out clean then the loaf is cooked.

Leave to cool in the tin for a few minutes, then turn out, remove the paper and finish cooling on a cake rack. Serve in slices.

Welsh Currant Loaf

This loaf lasts extremely well, especially if kept wrapped in clingfilm. *See photograph facing page 145.*

Making time about 5 minutes
Baking time about 1¾ hours

6 oz/175 g (1¼ cups) currants
6 oz/175 g (1⅓ cups) sultanas (golden raisins)
8 oz/225 g (2 cups) light muscovado (brown) sugar
½ pint/300 ml (1⅓ cups) cider
5 oz/150 g (1¼ cups) self-raising flour
5 oz/150 g (1¼ cups) wholemeal (wholewheat) flour
2 level teaspoons baking powder
1 egg, beaten

Measure the fruits and sugar into a large mixing bowl, pour over the cider and leave to stand overnight covered with clingfilm.

Heat the oven to 300°F, 150°C, gas mark 2. Grease and line with greased greaseproof paper a 2-lb/900-g loaf tin.

Stir the flours, baking powder and egg into the fruit mixture and beat well until thoroughly blended. Turn into the prepared tin and level out evenly. Bake in the oven for about 1¾ hours until well risen. Test with a warm fine skewer: if the skewer comes out clean, then the loaf is done.

Leave to cool in the tin for a few minutes, then turn out, remove the paper and finish cooling on a cake rack. Serve in slices spread with butter.

Cheese and Brazil Nut Loaf

Make this loaf with whichever nuts you happen to have in the store cupboard. I particularly like it made with Brazil nuts.

Making time about 10 minutes
Baking time about an hour

4 oz/100 g (1 cup) self-raising flour
4 oz/100 g (1 cup) wholemeal (wholewheat) flour
2 teaspoons baking powder
1 teaspoon dry mustard
1 teaspoon salt
freshly ground black pepper
3 oz/75 g (6 tablespoons) soft margarine
4 oz/100 g (1 cup) well flavoured Cheddar cheese, grated
2 oz/50 g (½ cup) Brazil nuts, chopped
2 large eggs, beaten
¼ pint/150 ml (⅔ cup) milk

Heat the oven to 350°F, 180°C, gas mark 4. Thoroughly grease a 1-lb/450-g loaf tin.

Measure all the ingredients into a large mixing bowl and beat well until blended. Turn into the prepared tin, level the top and bake in the oven for about an hour until well risen. A skewer will come out clean if the loaf is cooked.

Leave to cool in the tin for about 5 minutes, then turn out and finish cooling on a cake rack. Serve in slices.

Honey Teabread

Serve when freshly made with butter and honey.

Making time 15 minutes
Baking time about 1¼ hours

12 oz/350 g (3 cups) self-raising flour
1 level teaspoon baking powder
1 level teaspoon mixed spice (cinnamon, cloves, nutmeg, etc.)
2 oz/50 g (¼ cup) soft margarine
2 oz/50 g (½ cup) light muscovado (brown) sugar
4 oz/100 g (¾ cup) currants
3 rounded tablespoons thick honey
1 egg, beaten
¼ pint/150 ml (⅔ cup) water

Heat the oven to 350°F, 180°C, gas mark 4. Grease and line a 2-lb/900-g loaf tin with greased greaseproof paper.

Measure all the ingredients into a large mixing bowl and beat well until thoroughly blended. Turn into the prepared tin, level the top and bake in the oven for about 1¼ hours until well risen. Test with a warm fine skewer: if the skewer comes out clean then the cake is done.

Leave to cool in the tin for about 10 minutes then turn out, remove the paper, and finish cooling on a cake rack.

Date and Walnut Cake

Use fresh dates wherever possible rather than dried dates; they are less sweet and have their own distinctive flavour.

Making time about 10 minutes
Baking time about 1½ hours

> 4 oz/100 g (1 cup) self-raising flour
> 4 oz/100 g (1 cup) wholemeal (wholewheat) flour
> 2 teaspoons baking powder
> 4 oz/100 g (½ cup) soft margarine
> 4 oz/100 g (1 cup) light muscovado (brown) sugar
> 1 level teaspoon mixed spice (cinnamon, cloves, nutmeg, etc.)
> 8 oz/225 g fresh dates, stoned and chopped
> 2 oz/50 g (½ cup) walnuts, chopped
> 5 tablespoons milk
> 1 egg, beaten

Heat the oven to 325°F, 160°C, gas mark 3. Grease and line with greased greaseproof paper a 2-lb/900-g loaf tin.

Measure all the ingredients into a large mixing bowl and beat well until thoroughly blended. Turn the mixture into the prepared tin and level out evenly. Bake in the oven for about 1½ hours until well risen and a warm skewer comes out clean when inserted into the middle of the cake.

Leave to cool in the tin then turn out, remove paper and serve in slices.

Apricot Fruit Loaf Cake

A very moist loaf that keeps well for several days in an airtight tin.

Making time about 10 minutes
Baking time about 1¾ hours

> 7 oz/200 g (1¾ cups) self-raising flour
> 1 teaspoon baking powder
> 2 oz/50 g (⅓ cup) glacé (candied) cherries, chopped
> 5 oz/150 g (10 tablespoons) soft margarine
> 4½ oz/120 g (1 cup generous) light muscovado (brown) sugar
> 2 eggs, beaten
> 2 tablespoons milk
> 15-oz/425-g can apricots, chopped and very well drained
> 8 oz/225 g (1¼ cups) dried mixed fruit

Topping
> 4 glacé (candied) cherries, halved

Heat the oven to 325°F, 160°C, gas mark 3. Grease and line a 2-lb/900-g loaf tin with greased greaseproof paper.

Measure the flour, baking powder, glacé cherries, margarine, sugar, eggs and milk into a large mixing bowl and beat well until thoroughly blended then stir in the drained apricots and mixed fruit. Stir well then turn into the prepared tin and arrange the halved cherries in a line down the centre of the loaf. Bake in the oven for about 1¾ hours or until cooked. Test with a warm fine skewer: if the skewer comes out clean, then the loaf is cooked.

Leave to cool in the tin for about 15 minutes then turn out, remove paper and finish cooling on a cake rack. Serve in slices.

All-in-One Brioches

Serve these in place of bread rolls. They are made from a rich dough and are a bit between a cake and a bread roll. Delicious served warm for breakfast. I find it easiest to use the type of dried yeast you add directly to the flour. *See photograph facing page 145.*

Making time about 15 minutes
Proving time about 1¾ hours
Baking time about 12 minutes

9 oz/250 g (2¼ cups) strong plain (all-purpose) white flour
1 oz/25 g (1 tablespoon) caster (very fine granulated) sugar
2 oz/50 g (¼ cup) butter
½ oz/15 g easy-blend dried yeast
3 tablespoons hand-hot milk
2 eggs, beaten
a little beaten egg to glaze

Heat the oven to 450°F, 230°C, gas mark 8. Lightly grease 14 fluted brioche moulds of deep fluted patty tins.

Measure the flour and sugar into a large mixing bowl and rub in the butter until the mixture resembles fine breadcrumbs. Stir in the yeast until thoroughly mixed then add the milk and eggs and bind together to form a soft dough. Knead until smooth in the bowl then turn out on to a floured surface and knead well for about 5 minutes. Return to the bowl, cover with clingfilm and leave in a warm place for about an hour until the dough has doubled in size.

Knead the dough again on the floured surface for about 3 minutes. Divide the dough into 14 equal sized pieces. Cut a quarter off each piece, form the larger part into a ball and place in the tin. Press a hole firmly into the centre of the ball and place the remaining small piece of dough as a knob on top of this. Cover with a piece of clingfilm and allow to prove for about 45 minutes until light and puffy.

Glaze with beaten egg and bake in the oven for about 12 minutes until golden brown. Lift out of the moulds and allow to cool on a cake rack. Serve with butter.

Makes 14 brioches

Granary Fruit Scones

Scones take hardly any time at all to prepare and are always popular with friends when they pop in for tea. Scones should be eaten on the day they are prepared.

Making time about 10 minutes
Baking time about 10 minutes

4 oz/100 g (1 cup) granary (graham) flour
4 oz/100 g (1 cup) self-raising flour
2 level teaspoons baking powder
2 oz/50 g (1/4 cup) butter, softened
1 oz/25 g (1 tablespoon) caster (very fine granulated) sugar
2 oz/50 g (1/3 cup) dried mixed fruit
1 egg, beaten with milk to make 1/4 pint/150 ml (2/3 cup)
plus about 2 more tablespoons milk
a little milk to glaze

Heat the oven to 425°F, 220°C, gas mark 7. Lightly grease a large baking tray.

Put the flours in a bowl with the baking powder, then rub in the butter until the mixture resembles fine breadcrumbs. Stir in the sugar and the mixed fruit. Stir the egg and milk into the flour and mix to a soft wettish dough. Knead gently on a lightly floured surface and roll out until 1/2 inch/1.25 cm thick. Cut into 10 rounds with a 2½-inch/6-cm fluted pastry cutter, re-rolling the dough as necessary.

Arrange the scones on the baking sheet, brush with a little milk then bake in the oven for about 10 minutes until well risen and pale golden brown. Lift on to a cake rack with a metal spatula to cool. Serve with butter.

Makes 10 scones

Scotch Pancake Scones

Serve these whilst still warm, spread with a little butter.

Making time about 15 minutes
Baking time about 2–3 minutes

salt
lard for greasing
4 oz/100 g (1 cup) self-raising flour
1 oz/25 g (1 tablespoon) caster (very fine granulated) sugar
1 egg, beaten
¼ pint/150 ml (²/₃ cup) milk

Prepare a heavy frying pan by rubbing the surface with salt and then greasing lightly with lard. When ready to cook the pancakes, heat the frying pan until the lard is just hazy, then wipe off any fat with kitchen paper.

Measure the flour and sugar into a bowl, add the egg and the milk and beat until smooth. Spoon the mixture on to the heated surface in rounds, spacing well apart. When bubbles rise to the surface, turn the pancakes with a metal spatula and cook the other side for a further minute or so until golden brown. Place on a cake rack wrapped in a clean teatowel while cooking the remaining mixture, or keep in a low oven. Serve warm.

Makes about 10 pancakes

Right: Baked Alaska Birthday Cake (page 172).

Fast Granary Rolls

For lighter rolls, use half granary (graham) flour and half strong white (all-purpose) flour.

Making time about 15 minutes
Baking time about 10–15 minutes

> *1½ lb/675 g (5½ cups) granary (graham) flour*
> *1 packet Allinsons' easy-bake dried yeast, or Harvest Gold*
> *1 tablespoon sunflower oil*
> *17 fl oz/480 ml (2 cups) hand-hot milk, or milk and water mixed*
> *2 teaspoons sea salt, or a little less ordinary salt*

Grease two large baking sheets.

Put the plastic dough blade into the food processor and then add the dry ingredients and the oil. Process for a few seconds to mix them well. Then add the liquid in a continuous stream through the feed-tube while the processor is on, to mix the ingredients into a dough. Then process for a further 2 minutes so as to knead the dough. Turn it on to a floured board or surface.

Halve the dough and make each half into a sausage shape by rolling it. Divide each one into 12 equal pieces by cutting the dough through with a sharp knife. Shape the pieces into rounds by hand and place them spread out on to the baking sheets, allowing room for expansion.

Put the baking sheets into a warm place to prove, and heat the oven to 425°F, 220°C, gas mark 7. Bake the rolls, once they have doubled in size, for about 10–15 minutes, until they have browned on top and sound hollow when the base is tapped. Cool them on a cake rack.

Makes 24 rolls

Left: Jelly Tot Cakes (page 177).

ESPECIALLY
FOR CHILDREN

Most of these ideas are for younger children, as teenagers often like the same things as grown ups. The children can often help *make* them too. The greatest successes in our house were the Baked Alaska Birthday Cake (easy for me to whizz up too!), the Chocolate Chip Cookies and the Jelly Tot Cakes (tiny cupcakes made in sweet paper cases).

Baked Alaska Birthday Cake

I made this for Annabel's birthday cake earlier this year and instead of candles I served it with a sparkler burning in the top. She and all her friends thought it was wonderful. *See photograph facing page 168.*

Making time about 10 minutes
Baking time about 3 minutes

1 raspberry-filled Swiss roll (jelly-roll)
about 8 scoops raspberry ice-cream (not *the soft-scoop type*)
2 egg whites
4 oz/100 g (²/₃ cup) caster (very fine granulated) sugar

Cut the Swiss roll into 8 slices and arrange in a round on an ovenproof plate. Pile the scoops of ice-cream on top of the Swiss roll and put in the freezer whilst making the meringue.

Whisk the egg whites until stiff, adding the sugar a teaspoonful at a time. Take the ice-cream from the freezer and spread the meringue all over so that the ice-cream is completely sealed inside. Return to the freezer until required. It will keep in the freezer at this stage for up to 1 week.

To serve, heat the oven to 450°F, 230°C, gas mark 8 and bake the cake for about 3 minutes until just tinged golden brown. Serve at once.

Serves 8

Lemon and Cherry Buns

These are the sort of small cakes that are ideal to give as a contribution for a coffee morning.

Making time about 5 minutes
Baking time about 20 minutes

   2 oz/50 g (¼ cup) soft margarine
   2 oz/50 g (⅓ cup) caster (very fine granulated) sugar
   1 egg, beaten
   3 oz/75 g (¾ cup) self-raising flour
   2 oz/50 g (½ cup) semolina
   1 level teaspoon baking powder
   grated rind of 1 lemon
   3 tablespoons milk

Topping
   3 oz/75 g (⅔ cup) icing (powdered) sugar, sieved
   juice of about ½ lemon
   6 glacé (candied) cherries, halved

Heat the oven to 375°F, 190°C, gas mark 5. Arrange 12 paper cases in a patty tin.

Measure all the ingredients for the cakes into a mixing bowl. Beat well for a minute until thoroughly blended. Divide the mixture between the paper cases then bake in the oven for about 20 minutes until risen and a golden brown. Allow to cool on a cake rack.

For the topping, mix the icing sugar with sufficient lemon juice to give a spreading consistency. Spread a little on top of each bun and decorate with a cherry.

Makes 12

Mocha Buns

I'm not really too fond of paper cases but they are very useful if you want to take buns to a fête or on a picnic. I always stand the paper cases in a bun tin so that the buns keep a good round shape.

Making time 25 minutes
Baking time about 20 minutes

4 oz/100 g (1 cup) self-raising flour
1 level teaspoon baking powder
1 oz/25 g (1/4 cup) semolina
3 oz/75 g (6 tablespoons) soft margarine
2 oz/50 g (1/3 cup) caster (very fine granulated) sugar
1 egg, beaten
3 tablespoons milk
1 tablespoon coffee essence (extract)

Icing (Frosting)
1 1/2 oz/40 g (3 tablespoons) butter
1 oz/25 g (1/3 cup) cocoa, sieved
about 2 tablespoons milk
4 oz/100 g (3/4 cup) icing (powdered) sugar, sieved

Heat the oven to 375°F, 190°C, gas mark 5. Arrange 24 paper cases in bun tins.

Measure all the ingredients for the buns into a bowl and beat well for about 2 minutes until thoroughly blended. Spoon a good teaspoonful of the mixture into each of the paper cases and bake in the oven for about 20 minutes until well risen. Allow to cool on a cake rack.

For the icing, melt the butter in a small pan, stir in the cocoa and cook for a minute. Remove from the heat and stir in the milk and sugar. Beat well until smooth then allow to cool until a spreading consistency. Spread a little on top of each bun then leave to set.

Makes 24

Pineapple Buns

These are best eaten on the day that they are prepared otherwise the pineapple on top of the buns loses its shine.

Making time about 15 minutes
Baking time about 20 minutes

8¼-oz/234-g can pineapple slices
2 oz/50 g (¼ cup) soft margarine
2 eggs, beaten
4 oz/100 g (⅔ cup) caster (very fine granulated) sugar
6 oz/175 g (1½ cups) self-raising flour
1 level teaspoon baking powder
1 tablespoon milk

Icing (Basic Glaze)
4 oz/100 g (¾ cup) icing (powdered) sugar, sieved

Heat the oven to 350°F, 180°C, gas mark 4. Arrange 18 paper cases in bun tins.

Drain the can of pineapple, reserving the juice and one of the slices for decoration. Chop the remaining pineapple, drain well on kitchen paper then put in a bowl with the remaining bun ingredients. Beat well for about 2 minutes until thoroughly blended. Spoon a good teaspoonful of the mixture into each of the paper cases. Bake in the oven for about 20 minutes until golden brown. Allow to cool on a cake rack.

For the icing, measure the icing sugar into a bowl and mix with sufficient pineapple juice, about 2 teaspoons, to give a smooth glacé icing. Spread a little icing on the top of each bun. Divide the reserved piece of pineapple into 18 and use to decorate the buns.

Makes 18

Chocolate Cupcakes

When filling the paper cases try not to be too generous with the cake mixture so that there is plenty of room for the icing once they are baked.

Making time about 25 minutes
Baking time about 15 minutes

4 oz/100 g (1/2 cup) soft margarine
4 oz/100 g (2/3 cup) caster (very fine granulated) sugar
3 oz/75 g (3/4 cup) self-raising flour
1 oz/25 g (1/3 cup) cocoa
2 eggs, beaten
1 level teaspoon baking powder

Icing (Frosting)
4 oz/100 g plain (semi-sweet) chocolate
4 tablespoons water
1 oz/25 g (2 tablespoons) butter
6 oz/175 g (1 1/3 cups) icing (powdered) sugar, sieved

Heat the oven to 400°F, 200°C, gas mark 6. Arrange about 18–20 paper cases in patty tins.

Measure all the ingredients for the cakes together into a bowl and beat well until thoroughly blended. Divide this mixture between the paper cases and bake in the oven for about 15 minutes until the cakes are well risen and spring back when lightly pressed with a finger. Remove from oven and lift on to a cake rack to cool.

For the icing, measure the chocolate, water and butter into a bowl and heat gently over a pan of simmering water until the chocolate and butter have melted. Remove from the heat, beat until smooth and stir in the icing sugar until thoroughly mixed. Beat well until the icing is smooth. Leave to cool until just beginning to set then spread a little on top of each cake so that the top is completely covered with icing. Leave to thoroughly set before serving.

Makes 18–20 cupcakes

Jelly Tot Cakes

These tiny cakes are made in *petits fours* paper cases. They are so small that children can eat several at a time and seem to enjoy the novelty of them more than a large fairy cake or bun. My children enjoy helping to make these, particularly putting the sweets on top. *See photograph facing page 169.*

Making time about 20 minutes
Baking time about 15–20 minutes

  3 oz/75 g (6 tablespoons) soft margarine
  2 eggs, beaten
  4 oz/100 g (1 cup) self-raising flour
  1 level teaspoon baking powder
  3 oz/75 g (½ cup) caster (very fine granulated) sugar
  1 tablespoon milk

Icing (Basic Glaze)
  4 oz/100 g (¾ cup) icing (powdered) sugar, sieved
  about 1 tablespoon lemon juice

Decoration
  about 50 Jelly Tots (beans)

Heat the oven to 350°F, 180°C, gas mark 4. Arrange about 50 *petits fours* cases on baking sheets.

Measure all the cake ingredients into a bowl and beat well until thoroughly blended. Spoon scant teaspoonfuls of the mixture into the cases. Be careful not to over-fill the cases as the mixture will rise during baking. Bake in the oven for about 15–20 minutes until well risen and pale golden brown. Cool on cake racks.

For the icing, measure the icing sugar into a bowl and add sufficient lemon juice to give a spreading consistency. Spoon a little on top of each cake and spread out with the back of the teaspoon. When the icing has almost set, top with a Jelly Tot.

Makes about 50 tiny cakes

Chocolate Chip Cookies

Always a hot favourite in our house!

Making time about 15 minutes
Baking time about 10 minutes

 4 oz/100 g (½ cup) soft margarine
 2 oz/50 g (½ cup) light muscovado (brown) sugar
 2 oz/50g (⅓ cup) demerara (brown) sugar
 1 egg, beaten
 3 oz/75 g (¾ cup) self-raising flour
 3 oz/75 g (¾ cup) wholemeal (wholewheat) flour
 1 teaspoon baking powder
 6 oz/175 g chocolate chips

Heat the oven to 350°F, 180°C, gas mark 4. Lightly grease three large baking sheets.

Measure all the ingredients into a large mixing bowl and work together until thoroughly blended. Take teaspoonfuls of the mixture and arrange on the baking sheets well spaced apart. Bake in the oven for about 10 minutes until pale golden brown.

Remove from the oven and leave to cool on the sheets for a few moments then lift off with a metal spatula and finish cooling on a cake rack.

Makes about 32 cookies

Honey Fudge Cake

I wait until there are lots of broken biscuits in the bottom of the biscuit tin before I prepare this recipe: it's a good way of using them up.

Making time about 15 minutes

6 oz/175 g (³/₄ cup) hard margarine
6 oz/175 g (6 tablespoons) honey
8 oz/225 g (1²/₃ cups) currants
2 oz/50 g (¹/₃ cup) glacé (candied) cherries, quartered
2 oz/50 g (¹/₃ cup) raisins
12 oz/350 g (6 cups) digestive biscuits (graham crackers), crumbled

Heat the margarine and honey in a pan over a low heat until the margarine has melted, then increase the heat and boil rapidly for about 2 minutes, whisking all the time. Remove from the heat and allow to cool.

Measure all the remaining ingredients into a large bowl, add the melted mixture and mix thoroughly. Press the mixture into the bottom of an 8-inch/20-cm loose-bottomed round cake tin, and level out evenly. Chill in the refrigerator overnight. Serve in thin slices.

Happy Face Biscuits

This biscuit recipe can be used in a variety of ways, and I give here a basic and just a few suggested variations. You may like to use your own fancy cutters or add your own flavourings.

Making time about 20 minutes
Baking time about 12–15 minutes

6 oz/175 g (¾ cup) butter, softened
4 oz/100 g (⅔ cup) caster (very fine granulated) sugar
finely grated rind of 1 lemon
2 egg yolks
8 oz/225 g (2 cups) plain (all-purpose) flour
about 4 oz/100 g (¾ cup) currants
a little egg white to glaze
caster (very fine granulated) sugar to sprinkle on top

Heat the oven to 350°F, 180°C, gas mark 4. Lightly grease two large baking sheets.

Cream the butter with the sugar until light then gradually work in the lemon rind, egg yolks and flour. Knead until smooth then wrap in clingfilm and chill in the refrigerator for about an hour.

Roll out the dough to ⅛-inch/3-mm thickness and cut into rounds with a 3-inch/7.5-cm cutter. Arrange on the prepared baking sheets and use the currants to make a happy face on each biscuit. Brush with a little egg white, sprinkle with a little caster sugar then bake in the oven for about 12-15 minutes until pale golden brown. Leave to cool on the sheets for a few moments then lift off with a metal spatula and finish cooling on a cake rack.

Makes about 24

Variations
Make the dough as above, cut out into shapes with your own fancy biscuit (cookie) cutters then lift on to the baking sheets. Make a pattern on top of each with the currants, then glaze and bake as suggested.

Add the currants at the same time as the flour and work into the dough then cut out, glaze and bake as suggested.

Omit the currants and bake the biscuits plain without the glaze, then top once cold with a little lemon glacé icing (basic glaze) made with 3 oz/75 g (⅔ cup) sieved icing (powdered) sugar and about 1 tablespoon lemon juice.

Mallow Slices

When the children are home from school on holiday, and are fed up with amusing themselves, then get them doing some cooking. They love to have something to show for their time and effort.

Making time about 15 minutes

4 oz/100 g (¹/₂ cup) hard margarine
3 level tablespoons golden syrup (light corn syrup)
1 oz/25 g (¹/₃ cup) drinking chocolate
2 oz/50 g marshmallows, snipped into small pieces with wet scissors
8 oz/225 g (4 cups) digestive biscuits (graham crackers) crumbled

Topping
6 oz/175 g plain (semi-sweet) chocolate, melted

Line a shallow 7 × 11-inch/17.5 × 27.5-cm Swiss roll tin with a piece of foil.

Measure the margarine, syrup and drinking chocolate into a bowl and heat gently over simmering water until the margarine has melted. Remove from the heat and allow to cool slightly then stir in the marshmallows and biscuits. Mix well until thoroughly blended then turn into the tin and level out evenly. Press down firmly with the back of a spoon then chill in the refrigerator until firm.

Spread this biscuit base with the melted chocolate, leave to set, then peel off the foil and serve in slices.

Krispie Crunchies

Children adore these crunchies, and it's nice to include a couple in a packed lunch.

Making time about 15 minutes
Baking time about 25 minutes

4 oz/100 g (¹/₂ cup) soft margarine
3 oz/75 g (¹/₂ cup) caster (very fine granulated) sugar
¹/₂ egg, beaten
5 oz/150 g (1¹/₄ cups) self-raising flour
about 1 oz/25 g Rice Krispies

Heat the oven to 375°F, 190°C, gas mark 5. Lightly grease two to three large baking trays. Measure all the ingredients, except the Rice Krispies, into a mixing bowl and work together until thoroughly mixed and smooth. Take teaspoonfuls of the mixture and roll into balls and then roll each in the Rice Krispies. Arrange well spaced on the baking trays and slightly flatten each. Bake in the oven for about 25 minutes until just beginning to colour at the edges, then allow to cool on the trays for a few moments. Lift off with a metal spatula and finish cooling on a cake rack.

Makes about 18

Scots Tablet

The best way to describe this is as a more dry textured fudge. Very sugary so those with a sweet tooth will love it.

Making time 10 minutes
Baking time about 30 minutes

> 2 lb/900 g (4½ cups) granulated sugar
> scant ½ pint/300 ml (1⅓ cups) milk
> 6.91-oz/196-g can condensed milk
> 1 oz/25 g (2 tablespoons) butter
> 1 teaspoon vanilla essence (extract)

Measure all the ingredients except the vanilla essence into a large heavy pan. Heat gently until sugar has dissolved then increase the heat and boil gently for about 30 minutes until a light straw colour, stirring occasionally. Stir in the vanilla essence and beat for a few moments until beginning to turn sugary then pour into a lightly greased 6½ × 10-inch/16 × 25-cm Swiss roll tin.

Leave to set, mark into 96 small squares when beginning to harden, then leave to become quite cold. The squares will break off quite easily once the tablet is cold.

Makes 96 squares

Index

185